The Storytelling Artist

The Road to Controversial Art

Violence Politics Victims Police

IAN MACKENZIE

Disclaimer

Author; Ian Mackenzie Title: The Storytelling Artist

ISBN: 978-1-8381556-1-2

Category: Art, Self-Help, Business
FREEDOM Book Publishing

Book Interior and Cover designer: Hammad Khalid

For Connor and Tracy

The reason why I wrote this book

Contents

Foreword

I have had the pleasure of knowing Ian Mackenzie since the early 1990s when we were both police officers working in Cardiff. Since that time, I have witnessed Ian flourish in the various roles he has occupied and finish his career as the officer in charge of the National Assembly for Wales Policing Unit. This role was crucial in ensuring the relationship with the Welsh Government and Assembly and their officials was a harmonious one and it is testament to him that he successfully occupied this position for over 10 years.

It was during this period I would regularly meet him and discover that he was not just a good cop and martial arts expert but also had a real talent for art. That last discovery was made by accident, as one day I was having a coffee in the National Assembly buildings when I noticed some paintings on the wall, the subject matter, the colours and the message they were sending were all striking. I soon learned that Ian was the artist.

Whilst waiting for meetings I would often sit and chat with Ian and began to understand what drove him. It was clear that his family was his first priority, then came his other interests. I have to admit I was fascinated with his art and eventually commissioned a painting for myself. I will let Ian explain how that process went later on in his book!

This book and Ian's artwork enable us to better understand Ian as a person. I found the book a real pleasure to read as it gives a true insight into Ian's thoughts and feelings with an honesty that is refreshing.

Peter Vaughan

Lord Lieutenant for Mid Glamorgan

Retired Chief Constable South Wales Police

Testimonials

"What makes an artist? You could ask this question to many an artist and get a different answer but underlining most would be the one word - life. And in this book Ian Mackenzie gives an honest account of his and how it effects his art. A truly inspirational story of someone following his dream."

Gareth Hughes Broadcaster and Journalist

"With self- deprecating charm and wry humour, Ian chronicles events in his life which provided the inspiration for his art: - A Portrait of the Artist as a Young Man. It is part autobiography, part art guide, part glossy coffee table book. An innovative showcase for his prodigious photorealistic artwork."

Sian Williams LLB

"Ian Mackenzie charts his journey from shy schoolboy to professional artist with self-deferential humour and plenty of entertaining anecdotes. Ian inspirationally demonstrates how a determination to learn from the experiences that life throws at you, both good and bad, can feed creativity and bring success."

Susan Stratton, PhD

"This is a fascinating warm-hearted and candid account of creative development through life's experiences from childhood finger painting to incredible photorealism. Ian Mackenzie is a truly articulate artist in his prose and his paintings."

Laurence Kench BA(Hons) SSC HCA

"Vision, interpretation, preparation and a creative artistic feel has resulted in outstanding work. Each piece provides its own statement. They show the artist's view on world political and domestic issues. The 'I get it' response to each piece of work is a testimony to the artist's research, sensitivity and detail; coupled with dark humour and theatrical satire."

Stephen Rhys Williams

"Life's dark experiences can scar, restrain, illuminate and sometimes motivate a person to be a greater version of themselves than might have been. Ian Mackenzie in his new book - What makes an artist, tells his poignant story of how early adversity changed the course of his life. Swapping paintbrush for truncheon and back again, Ian paints a vivid picture of his life, a confused journey in a typically reflective and amusing manner that gets the reader turning the pages with a wry smile. It's a winner."

Jonathan de' Claire BSc (Hons) PGCE Dip Ed

"This is Mack's first published literary work and I hope it will not be his last. Seeing glimpses of those pivotal points in his life that have taken him to the very top of the tree in Karate, a senior position in the Police, success with his passion for painting and now an author was a delight. The experience was made better still by his of and reference to pieces of his own artwork throughout. He is a rare talent indeed."

Damian Stokes BSc. MRICS, Chief Executive, Rombourne Limited

Preface

Storytelling:

the **art** of telling a story using creativity, aesthetics, or communication to evoke, challenge and inspire. **Storytelling** is an **art** form and telling stories gives us a sense of culture, history, and personal identity.

Part One

An Introduction to My World

1

The Art of the Political Assassin

As I sat with bated breath watching one of the greatest calamities I had witnessed in the world of politics, I smiled wryly as the consequences flashed before me, one after another. Initially I could not believe what I was seeing. It just did not make sense. The whole world and its media were tuned into this very instant. The single most important moment of that person's career to date was about to be pushed to its limit.

How on earth could the huge mechanism that I knew all too well fail right in front of my eyes and go into meltdown? What I was witnessing would have ramifications for years to come. This was the real modern world at play, live and in your face, and many people would seriously be in the firing line for it.

It was conference time in the arena of politics and the Conservative Party legion had rolled up to the Manchester Central Convention Complex for their autumn flagship showcase. The security had been tightened and it was time for their leader, the Prime Minister Theresa May, to be introduced to a hall packed full of delegates.

A little after twelve noon on Wednesday 4th October 2017, she stood on stage, some twenty minutes into her first conference speech as the elected Prime Minister. Thousands of convicted die-hard Conservative delegates filled the venue, all eagerly listening to their leader's speech, which was intended to unify her beleaguered party to take on the political monstrosity of Brexit that lay before them.

I was barely three months into my retirement from a highly stressful thirty year career with South Wales Police. In the last ten years I had held one of the most contentious positions a person could have, balancing the critical role of policing within the complex and sensitive world of modern politics. I was the Inspector for the Police Unit housed within the National Assembly for Wales estate in Cardiff Bay, now known by its new name, the Welsh Senedd.

In that period, I had been responsible for the policing response to all incidents on the estate, the planning and successful execution of countless visits from high powered individuals, Prime Ministers, foreign leaders and diplomats and of course three Royal Openings by HRH The Queen. I was also well accustomed to the protests of many anti-establishment groups, the subversive nature of the counter-terrorist network and the occasional rogue politician. Throw them all together and welcome to my world.

So, it was of no surprise that I was interested to watch the newly elected Prime Minister in her role on the podium at her conference, paving her way for the next five years of leadership. The road had been rocky, calling for an early election, but she had made that choice and gone for it.

Events such as this are a likely target for groups or individuals to attack or protest against and require the highest levels of security. They take months of preparation in terms of the policing plan, ensuring it entwines with the requirements of the venue owners as well as the wishes of the conference hosts. Intricate planning is the key and a detailed and well-practiced operation will avert any type of breach of security and provide what we referred to as a 'safe venue' for all attendees.

I sipped my cup of tea and recalled the months of arduous planning that went into such events in the National Assembly for Wales with endless meetings, arguments and frustrations taking over my very existence right up to and beyond the moment of execution itself. Then, without a break, it was straight into planning the next one.

A warm glow of accomplishment enveloped me thinking of what I had achieved for many years, ensuring that Welsh politics had remained safe and all my energy and effort had been focussed on achieving that for the organisations that I had worked for and with. Now that I had left, it was time to reflect, appreciate the effort that others were putting into this moment, and move on to something new in my life. I shifted my position on the settee and got comfortable.

As the camera focussed dead centre on the Prime Minister, who stood behind the lectern reading her notes addressing the audience, a white sheet of A4 paper appeared from the right into the cameras view. The Prime Minister glanced at it as she continued with her speech. The person holding it reached up towards her, slowly stretching his hand out offering for her to take it from him.

She had dropped it I instantly thought. Naturally yes, that is what has happened, and this respectably dressed male wearing spectacles had retrieved it and is handing it back to her. Or it was probably one of her aides or the speech writer himself at hand with that very last amendment that will clinch the respect of the onlooking millions of viewers. Yes millions, staring at the piece of paper with the emblazoned P45 mark in the top right corner.

Oh my god, how on earth have they let this happen? It had dawned on me as the Prime Minister took hold of the paper. I could hear the words "Boris asked me to give you your P45". This guy was not a member of her team. He was not a delegate kindly helping her out. This was a breach of security that was going to have ramifications.

As anyone in employment in the UK will know that P45 is the code number on the certificate that an employer gives to an employee at the end of their employment. In other words, when you get the sack, you are handed this notification.

There, before thousands of delegates, live on UK television and being broadcast around the world was a guy giving the Prime Minister Theresa May her P45. And what is more, he said that he had been told by Boris Johnson to give her the P45. In essence, her notice to quit her job from a rival and potential challenger to her position as Prime Minister. It could not get worse.

I sat in disbelief, watching from the comfort of my lounge as the bare faced cheek of an individual embarrassed not only the Prime Minister and her party, but the Armed Protection Team around her, the policing operation and the venue security to boot. What a fiasco.

And then the penny dropped. This was not some spontaneous opportunity that an individual had seen and for a laugh, went for it. This was something that had been well planned, well thought out and had taken time to execute. There is no way this would have worked if it had been a random spur of the moment act.

This guy had been planning this for a long time. He would have had to gain a pass for the conference floor, perhaps applying to be a delegate months before. He would have had to see plans or the layout to know the routes and potential barriers and ticket points. He would have had to dress the part and not stand out and make sure at the security points his props were not recognised as items associated with a potential hoax.

I looked carefully at him as he turned to Boris Johnson saying that he had "done it" giving a thumbs up to Boris. The press immediately turned their focus in his direction away from the flummoxed Prime Minister on stage. Cameras clicked and videos rolled whilst some suited male person tried to get to him through the developing melee.

Look again I thought. He looks familiar. No one I immediately recognise from the list of anti-establishment members who had graced us with their presence at such events at the Assembly. It then clicked. He was not one of the usual suspects who we know to cause mayhem in this political media merry-go-round. It was Simon Brodkin, comedian and stunt prankster. I smiled. Well Theresa May, if you are not remembered for anything else, you will be remembered for being caught in one of the best pranks I have ever seen by the best in the business.

A couple of other people moved in around this now large scrum of media cameras, and Simon Brodkin was marshalled away from the front of the arena, into the aisle towards the rear of the hall. The crowds started to murmur and jeer, not knowing quite what had happened as the Prime Minister tried to repeat what she was talking about and her close allies at the front rallied, clapping and giving encouraging cheers for her to continue. The damage was done, and Simon Brodkin had done it.

My wry smile started to turn into a chuckle. It was rare that I witness something live on tv like that. Usually I saw the edited version hours later with a commentator's spin on the incident. My whole police career had been dedicated to keeping the peace, dealing with society's out of step individuals who did not comply with the laws, which in turn were set by the moralistic standard of those in power.

I laughed and I laughed. I was out of that race now. I knew from my experience the length of planning Simon Brodkin had gone to; I knew the length of planning that the police would have had to take. But that was one-nil to him I am afraid. I could not stop laughing at the bare faced cheek, the performance, and the result of what I can now call a fantastically executed operation.

I know he has done several stunts similar to this in the past such as getting on the pitch at Everton Football Club and warming up with the players prior to kick off. I had seen him join the England World Cup Squad at Luton Airport much to their amusement. And I recall him getting on stage at a FIFA conference and embarrassing Sepp Blatter at the height of the corruption scandal around the awarding of World Cup competitions to Russia and Qatar.

Turning to my artistic mind, I wondered what else Simon Brodkin had done. A plan started to formulate in my head as I looked into this comedian a little more. Over the next couple of weeks, I collated images and sketches as my artistic creativity came to the forefront. There was indeed something in this. A definite theme was starting to emerge.

My wealth of life experiences from childhood through to my previous profession of conformity, regulation, police operations, anarchists, politicians, royals, class differences, all coupled with my growing talent of creating paintings that considered figures, colour, light and shade, texture, art history and storytelling, were morphing into a single life of its own. The more I thought of it, the more ideas came to light and the deeper I found this subject took me.

The troubles that I had gone through to get to where I now find myself, stood for something. Every negative action that I had endured had shaped me for this moment.

Just like the artwork of the great masters of old that hang in the museums around the world, telling tales of great endeavour, of position and wealth, of trouble and strife, I also had a story to tell. My story of my background. A story like no other and I intended to tell it.

The painting "The Political Assassin" was born.

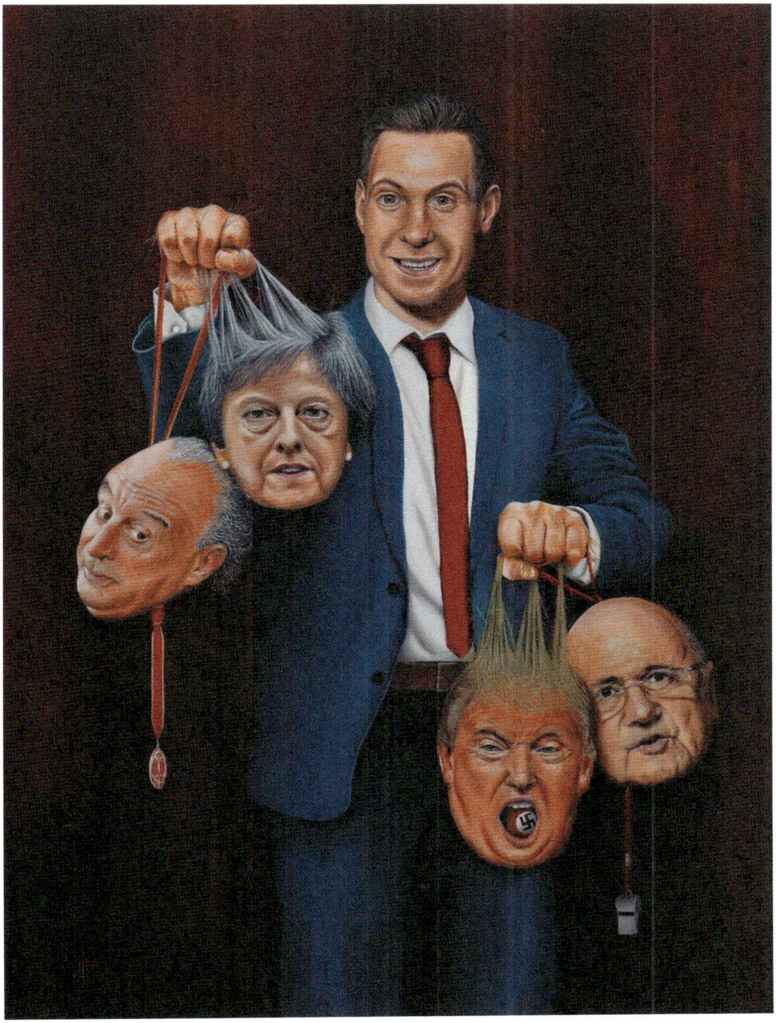

The Political Assassin 76 x 101cm by Ian Mackenzie

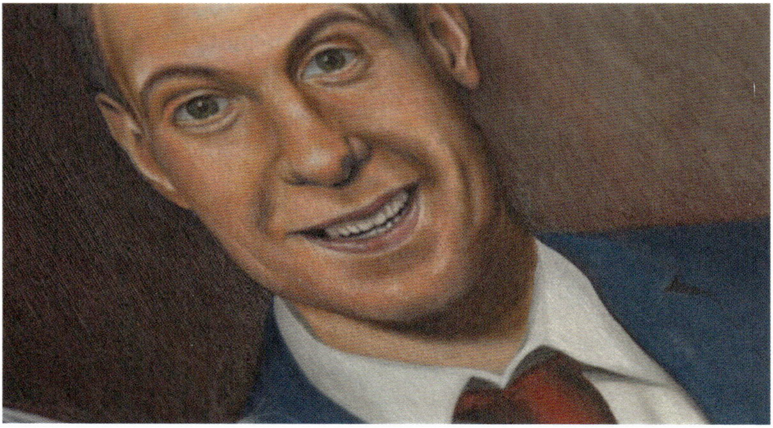

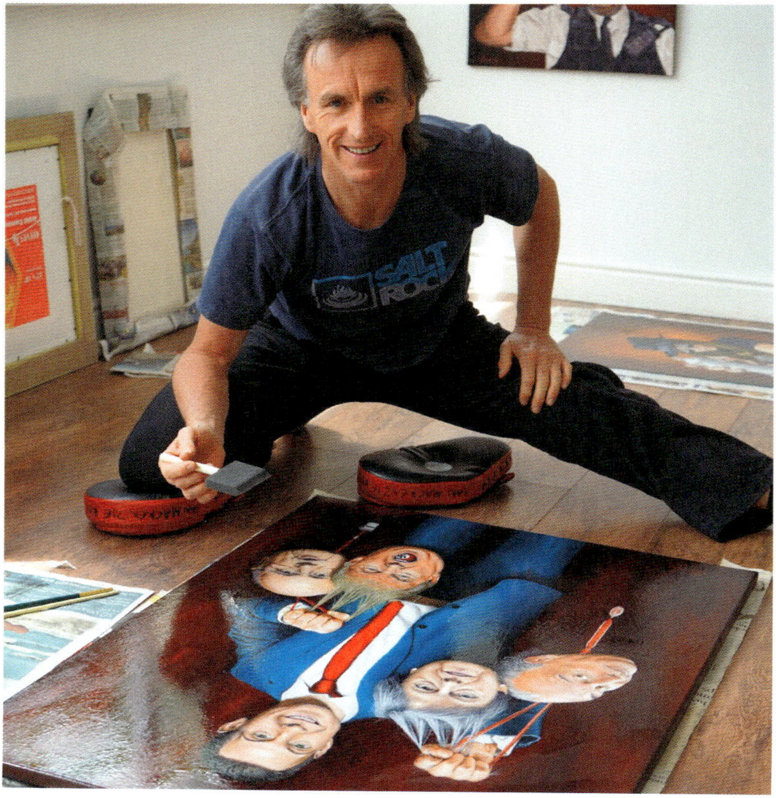
SALT ROCK

Part Two

Once Upon a Time

2

If You Are Sitting Comfortably…

"And that is where it all began" she commented, pointing at me in this photograph, stood in front of a guarded hearth in the living room of our small terraced house. Nothing unusual you may think. The typical child aged two years old, dressed in a romper suit from neck to toe, a plastic bib to preserve the clothing for longer than one meal. And a hat.

Nothing unusual at all. "It began right there, I'm telling you" my mother reinforced, indicating one of the twelve pictures in the new family calendar for all to see, her finger tapping the image.

"Yes Mum, thanks" I said. She tapped the picture again, letting the silence linger. The engaged group of family members gradually turned to see it. Slowly they all leaned forward as if by gravitational pull, they were drawn into the whirlpool towards the two-year-old, his romper suit and his hat.

There before them was not just the image of a small scrawny two-year-old child in an outdated 1960s onesie. There before them, was a young future charismatic Police Inspector, escorting and protecting members of the Royal Family, Prime Ministers and politicians, celebrities and high flying business executives, the movers and shakers of modern society, leading, influencing and subtlety managing politicians. A budding artist in waiting, soaking up experiences, anxious to create inspirational and controversial artwork telling the story of his encounters, of social injustice and controversy.

Or was the image just a picture of a scrawny two-year-old who had been told to stand still in front of the hearth, smile at the camera and moments before the flash bulb illuminated the dark smoke filled back room, had the latest child sized toy police helmet wedged on his head for a laugh?

I had no recollection of that photograph being taken which now formed part of my mother's present in the shape of a forthcoming calendar of embarrassing pictures for all to see. I had no recollection of any early urge to become a Police Officer. Even with Father Christmas leaving a Ladybird 'Easy Reading' book called 'The Policeman', it obviously wasn't entertaining me.

But getting hold of those things that made colourful marks on boards and paper, now that was different. As you placed the end on a surface and moved your hand across, there was a mark, a line or a shape. And if you repeated this movement back and fore, wow, something appeared in front of your eyes that you had done yourself. Now I remember that being really exciting.

This fledgling beginning in the world of art was one of my very first memories of what I can only describe as a fantastic childhood, full of fun, laughter, warmth and love. Of houses that were actually homes regardless of size and defects, and of childhood adventures that took me to endless exciting worlds in and around our neighbourhood.

My other memory at that age was of an incident that was not so fun and at the time caused a lot of trauma for those involved.

I was outside our terraced house with my mum, who was deep in conversation with the neighbour, so much so that she didn't really notice her two-year-old climbing the small garden wall. I recall that I had been told moments before "Don't climb the wall, you'll fall off," but not taking any notice, up I went. That was the only memory of that day.

Much to my mother's horror, I was taken to hospital by the family doctor who was urgently called to the house. Later that day, I returned home, the proud owner of a broken right arm in a cast and sling. I have no memory of the pain, the anguish, the doctor, or the resetting of the break.

Whether my memory of that moment of being told not to do something is ingrained in my mind due to the dire consequences of my action, or the fact that it has been talked about so much over the years that I couldn't possibly forget, is open to debate.

But memories do stay with you in some way, shape or form and can influence your decisions and subsequent actions which form the path you take and the people you choose to associate with.

And early memories were being formed in and around my activity with art and a creative streak was there looking for guidance and direction.

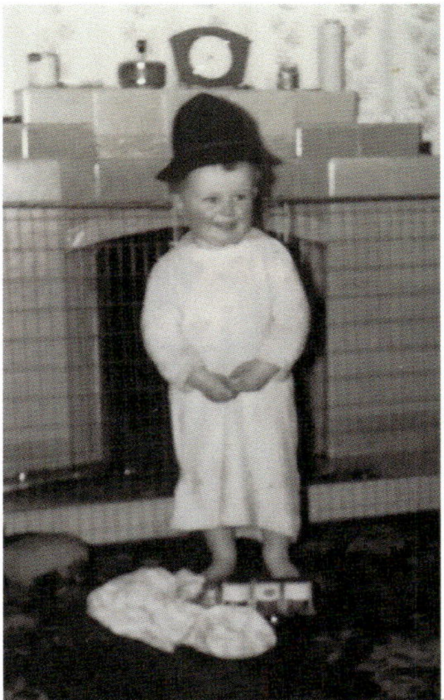

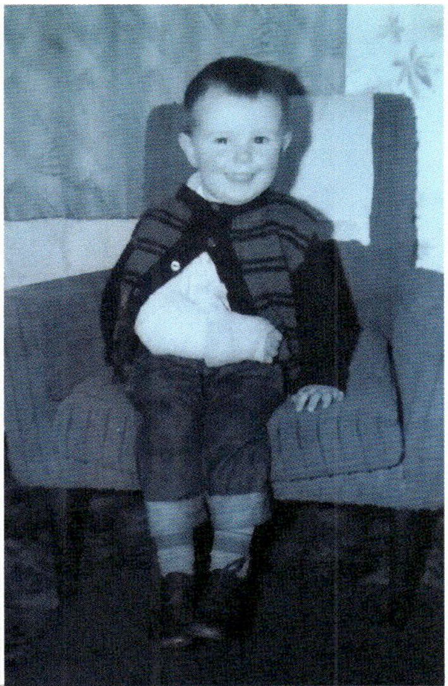

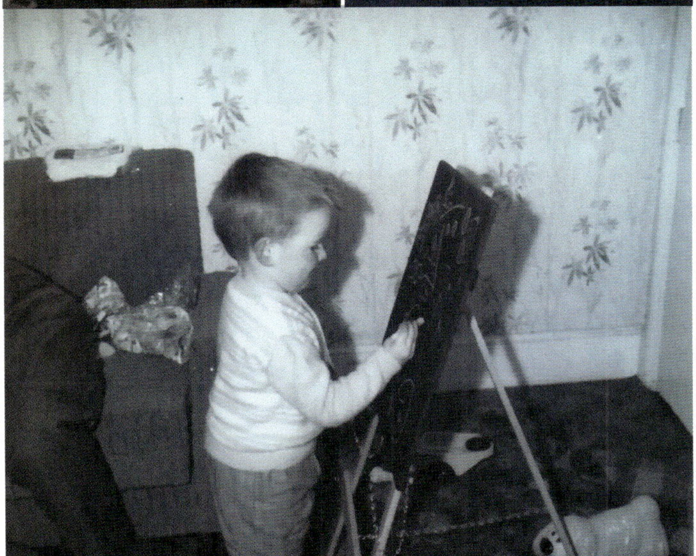

3

Growing Up and the Adventures of Drawing

My earliest recollection of entering an art competition was back in Victoria Infants School in my home-town of Penarth sometime in the early 1970s. I was around seven years old and can remember being ill and missing an art competition date. However, whilst off, my mother had told me that when I returned to school, I would still be able to enter the competition and I needed to think of some kind of picture to draw or paint.

So, feeling much better, I returned to school with my idea. I was placed in a classroom all on my own and left for who knows how long. It didn't matter, as I was going to be busy. I recall that the table was just the right size and I wouldn't have to stretch to get on top of my art pad like I would with the table at home.

By comparison to my living room in our small terraced house, the classroom seemed huge. So empty and so quiet, but full of colour and interest. It wasn't my usual classroom, and this was the first day back for me. Where was everyone I wondered.

Having been left to my own devices, I settled down and commenced my first ever competition masterpiece. I had an image of a cowboy in my head. Possibly one from those early experiences of Western programmes such as High Chaparral, the Lone Ranger or Casey Jones (which was later to be an amusing connection to my wife), all classic childhood entertainment, filling my mind with stories and adventures to act out straight after school when the Cherokees would be found near our neighbourhood stakeout.

I recall I was drawing on a piece of black paper and I was using some technique that I had practiced before which involved a lot of colouring as a base and then some rigorous scratching off.

I had no idea how long I had been drawing. I used to get absorbed in the moment, concentrating on nothing but the shapes, the colour and the story I was telling. It always seemed a bit strange that I could do art quite well and really enjoyed it, not knowing if it was because it was easy for me and therefore I didn't have to try hard, or because I just loved art itself and would try as hard as I could to create each picture. Either way, it was pure escapism and creativity.

Even at that early age, there was a story to tell, and when people asked me why I had drawn something, if I hadn't retracted through my shyness, I would articulate some elaborate story that was obviously so clear to me that in my mind there was no real need to ask.

But a lot of the time, that was where the stumbling block lay. In telling my idea, I had to speak to people and not being the most confident, my story was not being told. The lack of confidence was so much that I would even worry about going to friend's birthday parties. I would arrive there excited but then want to leave straight away. I was a nightmare for my mother.

My time was up, the competition over and the teacher returned to the empty classroom and solo artist. I presented my piece of artwork. The cowboy stood tall with his large dark hat, riding boots and shiny spurs. The cactus in the background was as big as the mountains behind. My story? Who knows? I couldn't speak to the teacher as it was a strange person! Did I win? Who knows!

I watched a lot of TV as a child. I was fascinated with it. The images, the action and of course, the story. It did not matter that it was black and white. What did matter was that The Lone Ranger fought to live another day, Batman and Robin sorted out all the baddies, and the occasional art competition thrown into the teatime TV mix was absolutely mesmerising.

I was astounded with the quality of the level of art and wondered if the kids that had entered were actually that age or had they got their big brother or sister to do it. Their pictures seemed awfully good. Most of the time I just watched and wondered what it would be like to have a picture on the television and everyone being able to see it. Wow, imagine that! An art picture of your very own on TV. How cool.

I knew I was encouraged very young to actively draw, no doubt to distract me from being a pain in my parents' backside. I also know that I didn't do that much painting. This was reserved for school time. Perhaps expense came in here, and the more costly of hobbies were avoided at home. Especially in the years following my seventh birthday when we moved to a house, which in my little world was as far away from my old haunting ground as the railroad stretched out across the Wild West in the exciting series programme Casey Jones.

However, I now had a massive bedroom at the back of the house, and the longest garden in the world backing on to the big boys' school which I would go to one day. The cost of the upkeep of this house must have stretched mum and dad to the limit as in my eyes, it was a mansion.

I recall there was usually some disastrous structural calamity waiting to sap up the coins which had been set aside for our weekly Saturday visit to Penarth's very first supermarket. If Lorna, my younger sister, and I were lucky, mum would purchase a massive block of Neapolitan ice cream. However, cracked roof tiles, no ice cream this week. Rising damp in the living room corner, no ice cream today. A warped back door... yes, you've got it.

Now, living in a mansion meant my artwork got bigger to match it. I was drawing on anything that I could get my hands on. I was even allowed to draw on the back of offcuts from rolls of unused wallpaper, and with a whole house to decorate, boy, there was no stopping this drawing artwork business.

Dinosaurs, cars, made up creatures, you name it, I drew it. I did have a problem with people though. I could draw them but most of the time, they were images closer to characters from a horror or sci-fi film that I occasionally got a glimpse of but was not allowed to see in full as I would have nightmares for weeks. Dr Who was bad enough, watching it from my usual hiding position behind the settee.

I would have my dad sat in a chair and try my best to draw him so that his legs were not as long as the last effort. His glasses were fine, but somewhere I had to put a pair of eyes behind them in his head which always ended up a make or break moment.

But drawing and copying shapes started to take hold and intrigued me as the world around me started to look different and exciting.

4

Miss Glaves and My First Exhibition

The image was so clear in my mind. I had no recollection where it had come from, but it was vivid as daylight. I pulled out the biggest art pad I could find, I sharpened my pencil and sprawled across my bed. The lamp on the bedside table was bright and illuminated the paper well. I had a small orange transistor radio which I would play at night under the sheets trying to tune into those pirate stations that I had heard of. I wondered what they would be up to tonight, fighting other ships and capturing treasure no doubt. It all sounded so exciting, if I could just find one transmitting on my radio, I'd know where they were burying their gold. I was ten years old.

I had the world before me and all that mattered was this image I had in my head. I started to draw this person riding a horse across the paper from left to right. It was a prince and he was accompanied by a woman. They had to get to the tower in the background as soon as possible. Hastily, I looked to draw the horse's head and body under the couple as the woman's dress billowed behind her with the speed they rode.

It was a great start. However, what I hadn't planned was that I had reached the edge of the paper and half of the horse's head was missing. I continued to draw further down the paper but again, I ran short for the legs.

Planning had not really featured to date in my artworld. Drawing was the important factor. And this drawing was something else. A couple in a dramatic situation raced to save the day. I couldn't start again, I was halfway through the adventure and it had taken me ages to get this far.

Armed with some cellotape and scissors I found downstairs, I commenced expanding the drawing by seamlessly joining pieces of the same paper to the bottom and the side of the artwork. A short while later, I was back in business, the cellotape had been secretly returned to the drawer downstairs together with the scissors in the kitchen, and I had returned, avoiding the creaking third step at the bottom of the staircase.

The quiet of the night ensued as the drawing expanded to capture the horse in full. Night after night, I would wait until no one stirred. Then, I would continue, pencil in one hand defining the shapes and shadows, transistor in other, listening out for word from a pirate and his scallys up to no good. I finished the drawing and proudly hid it back under a drawing board that my dad had given me for sketching in bed. Mission accomplished even though Blackbeard was still at large. These two horseback heroes would sort him out if he ever ventured to their tower.

I would often find that this was the best time to draw as it was peaceful, and I didn't have Lorna my annoying sister, hanging around poking fun and generally being good at what annoying sisters specialised in.

A few years later, when I had my own black and white TV in my room, which must have been quite some years later for such a luxury, I recall making a scientific discovery. I tipped the TV on its back, ripped a magazine page out, placed drawing paper on top of it, tuned the TV channel to absolutely nothing and wound the contrast to as white as I could. Hey presto, the best tracing image machine invented since Joe 90s amazing knowledge transferring machine. But for now, I drew what I saw, what I thought and added the skill of planning my pictures into the artistic framework.

As proud as I had ever been, I decided to take this in to show my favourite teacher Miss Glaves. I am sure that if there was anyone who would like it, she would. I had never met anyone outside my family who had been as kind and thoughtful as she had. She never criticised or told anyone off in school. How she got through the day with some of those naughty kids, I used to think was a miracle. She even played guitar to us on occasions which we all thought was really cool.

Such was her charisma and influence that it was not long before my classmate John Rook and I decided that we also wanted to learn to play guitar. Now John Rook was better than me at most things and playing this instrument was another of these examples. He was the only kid that I knew who was a Leeds United fan. I had heard of this legendary northern team when my mum would tut at the evening news glaring at a large group of fighting men outside some huge corrugated building. It was of course the away end of the Leeds United home ground Elland Road, and the visiting fans were being briskly sent on their way back south. But John Rook was not like that, he was a nice kid. He was my mate. He even owned his own full Leeds United home kit, socks as well. That was dedication and he was more dedicated to learning the guitar than I was.

I recall us at a church concert, waiting around in a narrow corridor with Miss Glaves to go on stage, guitars in hand after many hours of practicing the song Country Road. Nervously we recited the words over and over again, Miss Glaves reassuring us that we would do well and to just concentrate on her.

Suddenly, John Rook turned quickly, catching the body of her beautiful Spanish classical guitar, deeply scratching it with the neck of his. We all froze. However, she did not shout, she did not lose her cool or even show the slightest bit of annoyance. She just calmly reassured us and took us out onto the stage in front of the whole of Penarth.

Trying to teach us that song must have been a test of her temperament, let alone this incident that made us all freeze with shock just before our performance. Her beautiful expensive guitar was the furthest thing from her mind at that moment. She selflessly put our needs before hers and wanted to ensure that we were able to give the best performance that we could to all our waiting relatives.

So, considering how generous and kind she was to us all, I decided to trust to luck and take my newest piece of artwork in to class and show her quietly without anyone knowing. However, keeping this artwork to myself was the last thing Miss Glaves allowed.

After encouraging me to talk to the whole class about how I created the picture and tell what she said was a fantastic story behind it, she mounted the white paper onto a black background that made it stand out, and placed it on the wall in the classroom for all to see. She created one of those posh gallery signs with my name on it, just like those magnificent paintings in Cardiff Museum.

It was not only on the wall, labelled with my name on it just in case there was anyone left in my little world who did not know that I had created it. It was positioned in the corner next to the door, high enough that it could be seen through the window above the door and viewed by anyone in the adjoining hall outside our classroom. Any visitor who happened to knock on the classroom door, waiting to enter would stand and view my artwork. My drawing would be seen by more people than I actually knew.

I cannot recall why I drew this picture or what my intention was. There was no competition or homework to be done. I had this strange desire to just pick up a pencil and draw. Something inside me was starting to take hold of me and mould the way I drew, the way I thought and saw things, and the way I created pieces of artwork.

Miss Glaves was a true teacher in so many respects, encouraging and enthusiastic for creativity and learning. In a short school year with her, she left a lasting impression on me that is still with me today and hopefully, I have emulated her in the best way I possibly can.

5

First Day at St Cyres Comprehensive

At the start of September 1976, following the greatest summer a kid could ever have experienced, when the rain never came, the days never ended and the den in the garden got bigger and bigger, I walked down the garden path, out into the lane and turned right into the grounds of St Cyres Comprehensive School.

I was eleven and form 1KM beckoned. The hour had come to wear a uniform, pay attention, and become the small fish in a big pond. An excessively big pond with some very tall people as I recall and get reminded from time to time.

The little minnows of several primary schools like lost souls were being herded up the school drive towards a large aluminium framed set of glass doors. Turning right, we were shepherded into the largest hall I had ever seen in my entire eleven-year existence.

I recall finding my Victoria School friends and huddling together next to the longest set of curtains, as the hall filled with more and more similar groups until we couldn't move. Were there really that many kids in Penarth? Wow, where had they all came from? I had never been in one place with so many bodies.

And the uniforms. Everyone wore the same colour. My friends looked strangely peculiar, dour and starched, matching the stiffness of their newly ironed shirt collars. Ties were done up as tight as possible by parents and new black shoes polished to the extreme, all activities that would be part of the new morning ritual. Well, Dad is going to be busy I thought.

Suddenly, there was a loud booming voice from a giant of a man standing on the stage towering above us all. I was scared. So scared, I could not hear what he was saying. I kept asking myself what was going on, my friends giggling with their own nerves and excitement, whilst I froze.

One by one our little group started to disintegrate as the hidden joviality succumbed to the aura of authority that this voice exuded over us. We were being placed into orderly lines with an adult stood at the top of each line facing us. The voice still made no sense, even though my friends appeared to be adhering to its simple commands and walking away from our safe huddle to the back of the different lines.

The next thing I knew, I was nudged by a friend next to me. He pointed to the back of a line on the left-hand side of the hall. The silence was intense, amplified by a thousand eyes fixated on me as I started to walk across the floor to join the back of it. I could hardly move my legs. The fear spread through my body like the frost of an early January morning. I had no idea how many times my name had been called or how long everyone had waited for me. I was nervous to say the least.

Eventually after an eternity, we were marched single file out of the hall, down the longest corridor I had ever walked, and into the last door on the left. My shirt itched and my blazer twisted as the strap of my new satchel pulled my lapel across the tie that Dad had proudly knotted for me.

There before us was our home for the next year in Comprehensive School. Old wooden desks squashed together in three columns. A scramble ensued as we realised that this was all part of the dog eat dog fight for self-preservation. Don't sit at the front, don't sit at the back. The centre ground looked favourable I thought, as some kids from Fairfield Junior pushed straight past me clambering for the back, knocking me to the side of the centre column.

Bad move if you want to learn something, you may not be able to see the board I naïvely thought. Furthermore, as soon as that bell rang, I do not want to be at the back trying to make my escape for that promised land of my garden and my bedroom. Not so naïve, eh?

So, the centre of the room it is. The exact place where I was pushed, not standing out, not left behind. And with that, us Victoria Junior School pupils staked our claim.

6

Confidence and a Helping Hand

My lack of confidence played a huge part in my growing up at St Cyres. It haunted me and it made me stand out from most of the other members of my class. To this day, it still plays a big role in my life, worrying me as I attempt to forge a new career in the world of art, especially now that I had chosen to write a book and document not only my artwork, but also my struggle, to hopefully inspire others to try and achieve what they want. Yes, the lack of confidence had been making choices and decisions for me from a very early stage in my life.

I can recall many times when I was not able to speak in classroom situations due to pure fright. I could not put my finger on it, but I was god-damn scared out of my skin. I cannot believe that I actually got to where I am now, and I look back and wonder how I achieved it. How did I hold down a thirty-year career as a Police Officer when at the age of seven I couldn't even face being left at a friend's birthday party in a strange house?

I wonder how much my lack of confidence has shaped my life to date. Not being as sociable as others, I must have channelled my energy towards certain activities, for instance my creative side and my art. An early sign that this problem of confidence could grow in a positive direction.

After a few weeks of arriving at St Cyres Comprehensive at the age of eleven, I recall being sent to see Mr Roberts, the Head of the Lower School. I vividly remember sitting outside his office next to the teachers' Common Room. It was early in the morning, just after Assembly, and I had no idea why I was sat there.

I was racking my brain to try to understand why would I had been called to see such an important and authoritative person. In the few short weeks of being in this monstrosity of a machine they called 'The Comprehensive', I had not got into one bit of trouble. I kept my head down, I did my homework, I never talked to the other kids or get caught laughing at something one of the class clowns had done. And I had never given our art teacher, Mr White, the opportunity to throw chalk at me from the other side of the art room. He was a good shot as well and often flung a well-aimed white missile at the head of a young unsuspecting male lost to the world in a conversation and far removed from the day's crayon exercise.

The door opened and in I went. I was directed to the seat on the other side of what seemed to me the largest desk in the world. I had heard previously from my more mischievous mates that the cane was kept to the right, in the coat stand with the brolley. My eyes furtively attempted to locate it as I surreptitiously looked up whilst quietly answered a few innocuous questions, seeking some sort of sadistic reassurance to prepare myself that the cane was the reason I had been summonsed.

I knew absolutely nothing of Mr Roberts apart from the fact that he had taken us for a few lessons of French, and he had addressed us in Assembly. He was tall, well presented and carried an air of authority, one which you would not mess with. However, knowing nothing of him was not the reciprocal case.

To my amazement, he knew not only my name, which school I had recently come from, my current form and who I sat by in class, but he also knew that I had done well in very early English and Maths tests, I'd learned a whole page of Welsh words and the fact that I had already produced some pretty good pieces of art homework. We had only been there several weeks. My cards were marked. I've done something bad and I am in trouble.

I sat there, a quivering wreck, still no inclination as to what I had done. I answered his questions as best as I could waiting for the ultimate "and that's why you are here Mackenzie" with his left arm reaching for the cane in the coat stand. That would be my trigger to flee. The door was directly behind me. The small plastic chair I sat on would add as a barrier between him and me and I would push off with my hands, which were currently tucked under my legs sweating, trying to hide their involuntary shaking.

Both legs dangled under me not quite reaching the floor as I sat like Kermit the Frog halfway up the stairs in a Muppet Show sketch. I would run and run like I had never run before in my life.

I would run even faster than when I was aged six and late for my tea on a Monday evening which meant that I was also missing Batman as it followed the BBC news and Points West. My mother would bellow out of the back bedroom sash window across the gardens in the direction of the local small field, having dispatched me out of the front door earlier following school, telling me not to come back until I was hungry. Well I wasn't hungry, and now I was late for Batman. "Holy Cow" I cried, playing Batman's sidekick.

Yes, in my new found predicament in Mr Roberts office, Head of Lower School, I would run faster than I had ever run for any episode of Batman in my entire eleven year old life.

But strangely, I could not fathom out why my preparation for flight did not match that of the questioning that came my way. I mean, why would I want to run when this guy was talking about art and my drawings. Why would I want to escape when this person was interested in the airfix models that I had just told him about and the small soldiers I collected in abundance? This did not make sense.

I can't recall the end of the conversation, but upon returning to my class, a few inquisitive young scallywags wanted to know what that was all about, checking for the welt marks on my hands and the backs of my legs at the same time. I had no idea I told them, and that was the truth. I didn't.

The weeks passed and a few more of these chats took place as I cautiously found my way around new school life. Conversation with this figurehead became somewhat easier with me revealing that I owned a rabbit, played the piano and guitar and absolutely loved art classes the most out of all school life, even though it was a dangerous place with chalk flying left, right and centre.

Poor old Goggsy caught one in the side of the head last week. Mr White's aim was not as good that day as the mischievous target's neighbours were showered with a full box of chalk emptied similar to the gatling gun cutting down Mexican bandits in last week's black and white cowboy epic. Mind you, Goggsy's reactions were not known to be as sharp as others. His thick lenses were more of a protective shield than a sensory enhancement in this one way split second shoot out with Mr White.

The conversations with Mr Roberts came to a finale after a month with him promising that he would arrange for me, when of course I was ready, to play piano one Assembly. I left his company adulated that someone could think that I would be that important to be able to play and make others feel good.

I had better start taking my piano lessons a little more serious. Playing in front of all my mates and all those other kids, wow. I still could not get over how many kids there were in one location.

However, it was not long before my confidence problem started to dawn on me. To sit at the piano and play without making a mistake would be a challenge. The scenario played in my mind. I imagined the whole school waiting as I placed my music book upon the piano, shifting awkwardly as my underpants now rode higher than they had before, a result of form four boys going around randomly administering wedgy's to us unsuspecting form one new comers. If you ran and caused them the inconvenience of getting out of breath, when they caught you as they always did, your pants would be stretched so much, they were unwearable again. Explain that you your mother, which of course would bring about another raft of other repercussions, namely in the case of one friend, the embarrassment of a parent marching you up the school drive the following morning seeking retribution for your ripped pants. It was easier to accept a smack and be sent to bed early missing Scooby Doo.

The Assembly waited, everyone listening to the incredibly loud booming of my heartbeat, as I pictured myself approaching the piano for my forthcoming recital about to fill the hall with a melodic joyous sound.

No chance, no such chance. There is no way Mr Roberts would get me to even stand up and walk down the centre aisle of Assembly, let alone sit with my wedgied pants on another tall seat, legs dangling, feet not able to reach the floor, playing a rendition that would make Les Dawson's comedy piano sketch sound promising.

No. Confidence was an issue and it was not going to go away. It would continually win its battle, slowly chipping away, being reinforced by the callous, vindictive bullies and oppressors in life and those who have a lower expectation of you and for you, keeping you where you belong, below them.

When I think back on those conversations, I accepted them for what they were. No more than a chat with this nice person who was interested in me. As an adult, on occasions I thought about these and realised much later, that somehow, someway, I had been singled out and identified probably for my reluctance to engage in the classroom environment. This I guess, was an early form of counselling from a person who in his way had decided to give me a helping hand to allow me the opportunity to feel better than I did in that environment, to stand equal to those around and be afforded the chance to take what I needed from the situation and make life a success.

I never told my parents of these meetings for the fear that I would be asked a barrage of questions that I could not answer, as at the time I had no idea why I was there. Only now on reflection, I understand there are actually some nice people looking after your needs at certain times in life, even if you don't recognise this when it happens.

Mr Roberts was one of those people who from back in the shadows, steps forward when someone falters, when justice fails, when off the beaten track becomes constantly worn, and through their gentle kindness and positivity, guides and reassures those lost souls, only to silently fade once more into the background when the job is done, to wait for the next calling.

I hope to be one of those true heroes someday.

Form 1KM St Cyres Comprehensive 1976

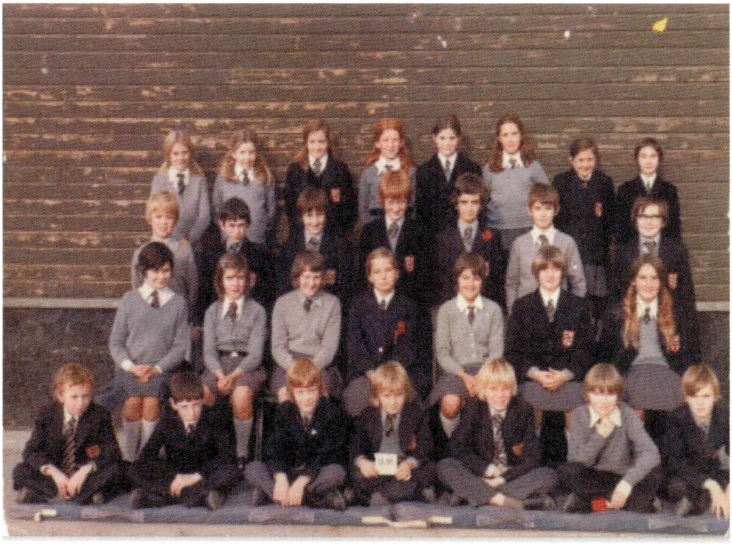

From the top, I am 2nd row, 3rd from left

Part Three

Scarred and Scared

7

There is No Future in Art

Art classes were fantastic in school. What an escape from boring English Language, French and Welsh. Maths wasn't too bad, Geography ok, Technical Drawing better, but Art was the best. It was as if there was a freeing up of your mind, a removal of all the restrictions and you could do something that didn't really have to conform with much. It was a different thought process that I was starting to understand. I recognised that there was a place for conformity and direction as these traits helped you learn large chunks of information speedily.

But art was unique, it was a shame that our art lessons were no more than two hours a week, because it was also a scream.

As we advanced through the terms and subsequent years in school, we were exposed to new learning experiences. Art had moved on from just painting to working with clay, something totally different from normal lessons. Mr Farmer our art teacher was showing us how to make simple shapes and small pots out of a dollop of clay and water. It was nothing like the TV image of the potter on a spinning wheel creating a beautiful tall vase with a delicate neck. Far from it. We were lucky to get anything higher than two inches without it disintegrating before us in a wet ugly heap.

If we were able to get further than this first stage, the big issue that we faced (besides the lack of skill), was that if we didn't work the clay enough, it would hold air pockets within it which would heat up in the kiln and explode. Numerous times that term, we would return to the class a week later, eagerly awaiting the kiln to be opened to find half of the classes work chipped, maimed or totally destroyed. So, week after week, it was back to starting again for most of us whilst the lucky ones got to paint and glaze their obscure pots and shapes that formed presents for adoring family members.

Perseverance prevailed and we started to get better with a greater number of artistic pieces surviving each week. However, my mate and I were bored with this. We had been trying to master this art for the good part of a whole term and no matter how hard we both tried, our success was in the hands of someone else who didn't bother or try as hard as us. We wanted to be in control of our own success, not in the hands of these half-witted buffoons. I had a plan.

I pointed out to him that if our clay objects were unfortunate enough to hold unwanted air within them, there was a chance that they would fall victim to the heating process and explode. Not only that, if there was enough air involved, they may very well take out other clay and if they contained a great amount of air, well who knows what could happen. We thought about it and giggled.

Why not? We thought, time to put a secret plan together and, under the guise of creating Grandma's pending birthday presents, we tested our theory. Our creations were like no others. The care and the meticulous preparation that went into them was unique. We smiled and moulded as we created air pockets throughout the whole clay. It was an artform all of its own. We both lined up outside the drying cupboard with fellow classmates smiling and saying to each other "Your Grandma is the luckiest in Penarth" bursting into laughter as we placed our beautifully sculpted pots on the shelf.

A week later we returned. We all sat in our respective seats as Mr Farmer settled us down. He explained that unfortunately, just as we had all started to perfect the skill of pottery, this week's drying process had taken its toll on our work. In fact, it was so bad that no one's work survived.

I couldn't believe it. I had to bow my head instantly, placing my forehead on the group table and covering my face with my hands. What success! It must have sounded like I was mourning, god knows how I managed to disguise my laughing and delight. I peeked at my mate next to me from between my hands. He was slyly looking back at me, better at holding his surprise than I was. The whole class had turned towards me as Mr Farmer's voice asked if I was ok. My mate quickly replied "Its ok Sir, it was for his Gran for her birthday. He'll be alright."

As Mr Farmer looked away, my mate dug me in the ribs making me jump. "We did it, we made a massive explosion," he whispered excitedly, and we laughed, partially hiding our victorious elation from everyone. We left school that day excited with our newfound hobby.

A full term of this activity was coming to an end and Mr Farmer had decided that we had reached a level that we should make some pottery to sell in the school fete in a few weeks' time. He was always very optimistic, despite the setbacks that the kiln drying process threw up and the misfortune that befell the budding potters in our class.

So, again, we sat and created pottery items once more. We could make whatever we wanted. I chose to make an animal and used the technique of rolling the clay into a thin sausage like shape and wound it around to make the body, filling the gaps with extra clay, sculpting its torso. I added the usual amount of our special ingredient and proudly presented my product at the end of the afternoons lesson. My mate did the same and again we lined up at the drying cupboard overtly admiring each other's craftwork and future grandparents' presents.

The week passed and we found ourselves back on the first floor art room of the old school block. Mr Farmer admitted that he had only put the items in the kiln the evening before, so the class clambered forward to see the unveiling. My mate and I casually sauntered over behind everyone as the door opened. Everyone's anticipation was replaced with a groan of dismay and disappointment. Mr Farmer acknowledged the failure and started to empty the kiln. I looked at my mate, he winked. Another successful mission.

All of a sudden, Mr Farmer reached further into the kiln. "Oh wait, we have something here" and he retrieved three items of pottery. We all turned and looked. Three out of twenty-five totally intact. He looked victorious. At least there was something to sell in the school fete.

Two pots and a pig. Two fairly round small pots and an ugly looking pig with a lopsided face and one ear. I looked again. My mate stared and turned to me. I reached forward and placed my hands around a piece of surviving pottery.

The scene was biblical. I raised the item like the chalice from the last supper. My pottery, my artwork, my pig. It had defied all odds, even the odds that I had created within itself, and survived. Everyone looked in awe at the ugliest piece of pottery ever created, formed with no regard to appearance whatsoever. Frankenstein's pottery. My mate nodded bemused and bewildered. Yes, my pig was biblical.

Some forty-two years later, my pig stands proudly in the lounge cabinet alongside expensive ornaments and trinkets. He occasionally makes an appearance from behind his hidden position when I am daring enough, and cheek allows. But it is not too long before he gets returned to its place in the corner partially out of sight from visitors. He is misshaped, ugly and has a dark brown patch on his backside. However, he is mine and I am proud of him, where he came from and how he came to be.

School slowly progressed in some way, shape or form. My confidence grew and waned. I was good at some things and terrible at others. I was nothing special. I tried my best in most subjects, but I did love art. It was such a release from the restrictions that tied you down. However, with the impending O Level exams around the corner, we fifteen and sixteen year olds needed that conformity to ensure that we could regurgitate all that information onto those exam papers pretty soon. I faced the daunting aspect of nine O Levels. All I had to do was to remember as much as I could, submit my telephone kiosk model for my Design, Craft and Technology course and throw a bit of paint on some cheap school paper in a practical for Art, and I would be home and dry for the summer of all summers.

I soon reached the point when nearly all of my exams were out of the way and I just had my seascape for Art to put together. I had the choice of collage or painting. I never really got the whole idea of collage art that some pupils did so enthusiastically. I always thought it was a cop out creating most of your picture out of cuttings from your Mums old Kays catalogue or Women's Weekly magazine, fitting them together like some crazy 1970s psychedelic album cover and hey, I am an artist.

I was a few days away from finally finishing my exams. I was in my Art practical and I had one more exam to go. The land of summer, football, girls, my bike, and nothing more important than enjoying myself was beckoning. Mum and Dad had split up and my head wanted to explode. I wanted to run and run until there was nowhere else to run. I had made my choices for next year and with a bit of luck, they were all in the bag so to speak. Just one Art exam and I am out of the door with my future sorted for two years in the sixth form.

Ah Mr Farmer, my Art teacher waiting at the door as I placed my brushes in the drying pot, picked up my four-year-old satchel and placed my final piece on the front desk. "Hopefully, this one will set you right for your A level course Ian" he commented as I acknowledged him whilst leaving the art room.

"Oh no Sir. There is no future in Art. I'm doing Maths". Well, if there was a moment in my life which taught me to think before I spoke, it was then. I would not say I was the star pupil of the class, there were plenty of them, but I would like to put myself above those who fitted perfectly into the well-known 70s phrase 'clay class'. Those who would not only test the patience of any teacher to their limit, but also test the flavour of every paint product made available to us. One only had to look at some mindless grinning blue gummed individuals to see exactly where the missing paint had disappeared today.

But as far as Mr Farmer was concerned in that split second, I am pretty sure I had been reclassified, relabelled and removed from any future personal fondness for my methodical process of creating acceptable artwork.

"And whose decision was that?" He snapped at me. As sure as innocence is, my reply just made things a whole lot worse for my early escape from school. I mean we were in the middle of Wimbledon and I had endured exams in History, Maths, English Language, English Literature, Welsh, (don't get me started on Welsh. In fact, I don't think I did get started on it. The only class I ever got kicked out of was Mrs Peate's Welsh class, that is about as good as it got for me).

"The Careers Advisor Mrs Stanton told me there was no future doing Art. There are no jobs in it, and I should go and join the RAF or something like that, Sir". Having now blocked my early escape, my mates passed me giggling, sticking their two fingers up at me behind Sir's back from the corridor outside, I was doomed.

"Wait there, young man. We shall see what future there is in Art" he replied,

and as his fury started to manifest itself into a raging tornado, he spun on the spot almost catching the clay class dance crew behind him with their familiar offensive sign language, trying to blend into the pale cream corridor walls.

"Run, run before he comes back. We've nicked paint cubes to bomb the caretakers". Life on the edge with the clay class members, running from the very teacher who had told you to stay. Who was going to be marking your O Level exam, I thought?

I looked at my mates disappearing down the stairs, thinking they were already part of the reason why we could only paint in specific colours at certain times of the month. Where are the missing colours? Oh yes, all over the roof and up the side wall of the caretaker's house on the driveway out of school. No, I was not going to run.

And what did he mean? What future there was in Art? Mrs Stanton knows best. She tells everyone how to get a career, how to get a job and earn money. Mr Farmer tells you how to draw and paint and escape from all those busy, stressful life activities. It is only supposed to be a hobby. One that I happen to be able to get a qualification in. Anyway, I don't know of any artists who have a job as an artist. Yes, there is Mr Maggs, but he paints houses. Of course, there is Mr Farmer and Mr White. God knows how he is an artist. Perhaps he is not. He is a pretty damn good chalk thrower. My god, he can hit a talking kid's ear at twenty yards in a full room. Well, most of the time that is.

What Mrs Stanton says, Mrs Stanton knows. She is the expert. Anyway, I might fancy flying a jet plane when I am older. Not sure about the grey uniforms though, they are a bit drab. And I'll have to get a short haircut. I'll have to have my Rod Stewart spikey doo flattened. Not sure about that too. Maybe I had better think about this a little more.

Right now, it was the end of the day and he had not come back. It looked like most of the school had departed. My class certainly had. OK I'm off. With that, I left the school Art classroom for the very last time, excited to have almost finished my exams, especially my beloved Art, but confused as to my future and the conflict that it seemed that I was wrapped up in.

Little did I know that conflict was about to get a whole lot worse and eventually dominate most of my life.

8

Tonight's the Night

Some people are able to recognise a moment or a period in their life when everything changes for them and they start on a different path. Some people don't see it until a short while later when the change has taken them off in that new direction, while for others it's not until much later in time that they look back at what they've done and see the pivotal moment that triggered the change or changes that subsequently created their fate.

There are so many influences and events that mould our environment that can change the path we take through life. Some influences we chose to be exposed to; some we have no choice. The inspirational speech, the kind gesture, unintended misdirection, poor advice given and taken, the sporting figurehead, the song lyrics, lust, greed, poverty, spiritual belief, an act of courage - all give the opportunity to affect our fate.

It is what you do about those influences and how you let those changes define you that will make you the person you ultimately become. The first instance of directional change for me had taken place. The second was just around the corner. I was in the thick of change and I had absolutely no idea.

I had moved on from my art studies in school and was focussed on getting through the sixth form with good enough A Level grades to get me off to some university somewhere. Why not? Everyone was talking about these places and it would certainly be a pit stop before the sage Career Advisors' truth came to fruition and the Royal Air Force drags me into the career others had chosen for me.

A Levels were different to O levels and required a separate type of thinking and approach. I was creative, I knew that, but my creativity did not really fit in with Maths. So that subject soon got replaced with Law which did not really sit well with Geography and Geology. But what was I to know? I had been guided away from the subject that I loved, the easiest subject I could do, and put on a path of mild confusion and bewilderment. I think back and wonder how many other teenagers were given poor advice, took ill-fitting subjects and were just left, shoehorned into the state system to get them out at the other end with as little disruption as possible.

So, sixth form had its ups and downs. It also had its parties, which were becoming more and more enjoyable as my mates and I were starting to experience alcohol as we closed in on our seventeenth birthdays.

Parties were being organised at local venues quite regularly. The venue would have to be hired by someone's parents, so you either needed parents with money or to know someone who had. My parents did not have money, so it was down to me and my kooky mates to get accepted and in with the crowd.

There were are few local party places in and around Penarth, such as the Marconi Club, the Sea Lion and Pegs. Sometimes we ventured into Cardiff City Centre but had to rely on our parents for lifts to return after the train network closed. Those kids with richer parents owned their own cars and as such went everywhere and became the party goers of the sixth form. I did not own a car, far from it, and neither did my mates, but we did get to a lot of the parties and we did experiment with the different alcoholic beverages, pocket money allowing.

One party in particular was earmarked on my calendar on the back of my bedroom door. It was at the nightclub on Penarth Pier, a venue called Pegs. I could not remember what the occasion was, but I was going to do my best to get to it as it was obviously so important that I'd written this date on my sacred Hazel O'Connor calendar!

A few months earlier, John Rook and I had gone to see Hazel O'Connor perform at the Top Rank nightclub, Cardiff. Wow, what an experience! Somehow, someway, I have no idea how, we ended up backstage and met the band, with one of us taking photos. I think it was me with my Kodak Ektra 'with steadying handle', but I cannot be certain. I just remember the surrealness of the moment.

I did not sleep that night. I was so enthused by that experience, I just had to create something. I reached for my art pad and drew what I thought was a fantastic sketch of the star of 'Breaking Glass' herself. This was later followed by a series of sketches of other musicians, including Toyah, David Bowie and of course Rod Stewart.

John Rook and I finally met Hazel O'Connor when she came to John Menzies shop in Cardiff promoting her book, and we queued for most of the morning to get an autograph. We dressed appropriately with our mohair jumpers, skinny jeans, and our spikey hair.

I carried all three of her albums that I had dutifully bought upon their release. I even had a single record which I asked her to sign for that girl in my class named Tracy Jones who still had not acknowledged my existence. A signed record, it has got to work, surely. Now that was entrepreneurial love!

Dressing appropriately made sure we felt like we fitted in with where we wanted to be in our society. In it but outside of it. It was important. This was the way. To stand out and be different from the rest of the crowd was an expression of individualism which I missed in not taking art further in the school curriculum. So, my expression was through my look.

I could not say I was a true punk or even a fully-fledged heavy metal fan, even though I went to the gigs with my different sets of mates and loved both styles of music. Wearing punky New Romantic-style clothing to heavy metal gigs was a laugh. I was, however, a true Rod Stewart fan at heart and I knew I was the only male in the school to hold this accolade. As did everyone else. I was proud of it and I loved his music. I didn't care about being different.

A party at one of the local venues was an opportunity to dress up like a Cheshire cat and impress the girls. Well, it worked for all those rock legends on Top of the Pops, it may very well work for me.

I had been to Pegs once before that fateful evening in November 1981. I recalled that the exciting part of the evening started at 9pm with the DJ playing the theme to the original TV detective show, Hawaii Five O. That was the trigger point to hit the dance floor and strut your stuff. Then, it was a free for all to try and get the DJ to play your type of music more than others.

My dress for the night was the best I could muster. A tight pair of blue jeans with a white piping stripe down each leg that were so tight, there was very little room for anything in your pockets except coins for beer and your front door key. These jeans slotted well into a pair of red suede ankle boots, adorned with several buckles and no grip whatsoever in the wet. And finally, the piece de resistance. My brand-new red dinner shirt with a frilly front piece to make even Adam and the Ants look averagely dressed.

I was it. I was there and I knew it. My close mates had come to expect such outlandish clothes. Hey, well it was the rise of the New Romantic fashion after all and I was a David Bowie fan. I did draw the line at dressing like the front cover of his album Scary Monsters though. I have limits. Well, income restrictions more to the point.

So, tight blue jeans with white stripes, red velvet boots with buckles, a big red frilly shirt and the theme to Hawaii Five O indicating it is dance time. What could possibly go wrong?

With a pint of bitter beer in my hand, I returned from the bar to where we were all sat overlooking the colourful array of eclectic St Cyres Comp sixth formers, accepting each other's differences and tastes, hitting the dance floor for an enjoyable escape from lessons.

I manoeuvred around a couple of people I didn't recognise to try and reach my seat. However, the gap that had been there just a moment before I glanced towards the dance floor had disappeared. I moved to the side, but that gap disappeared too. So did the gaps to each side and behind me. What on earth was going on? I know that I had drunk a couple of pints of beer by that stage, but I did not think that it was enough for me to lose all sense of space.

With that I felt my body jolt from one side to the next. My beer was starting to spill and I recall apologising. To whom, I have no idea. I could not see my friends who were there in abundance, just a group of strangers, taller than me, broader than me and older than me.

I looked at the one directly in front. I could not hear what he said. His lips moved but the disco was cranking up. I needed to get to my seat. The night was young, and a lot of enjoyment was planned. Politely I said sorry to this person as I could not hear him, and I leaned forward to clearly understand what he was saying. He probably liked my shirt. It was a one-off and of course, no one else had one like it, especially with matching boots. He wanted to know where he could get one. Yes, that was it.

As I leaned forward and looked up to him, the room went dark. A strange loud noise cracked out over the whole of the disco drowning the music. A noise that exploded in my head and shot pain into my eyes. Lights started to flicker from the darkness as I felt the pressure of someone behind me hit the back of my body. Lucky there was someone to bounce off I thought.

Slowly but surely, it dawned on me. My newly found fashion friend enquiring about my dress sense was not really interested in where I had purchased my shirt. Or my boots for that matter. In fact, this new friend was not interested in anything I had to say. He just looked down at me and grimaced as I started to realise what had happened.

Blood ran down my nose and dripped onto my hand that still held what was left of my pint of beer. I had been head butted in the face. And come to think of it, punched in the back, just to even out the backward trajectory that I had been heading in from his other fashion admirer. The further two assailants each side stopped me from escaping from my new group of special mates.

His grimace turned into a smirk as he leered down at me waiting for me to do something. To be honest, I was shell-shocked. I had no idea that this was going to be my special night, and that these were going to be my new best bigger and older friends. I could not say anything as I tried to fathom the numbness that started to spread across my face.

All of a sudden, the group roughly parted and I was knocked sideways as they passed me to disappear somewhere and congratulate each other on this great victory. Round One.

I stumbled to my chair reaching for a handkerchief, the other item that thankfully just about fitted in my jeans pocket. Mates huddled around me with worried looks on their faces. Questions flew at me whilst a few kept looking towards the bar where this gang now stood laughing and praising each other.

I could not answer any of them as I had no idea why it had happened, who they were or what I was going to do. My mates looked worried. I felt sick. Word went around the nightclub quicker than Rizzo's pregnancy rumour in the film Grease. Everybody knew that I had been attacked.

I mopped up the blood from my nose and had a drink. I had not spilt all my beer, that was one good thing. I just hoped that I do not look too bad. No chance of a slow dance and a smooch tonight. No, impossible. Not with these nerves that had started to kick in. My hands were shaking, my legs feel weak. I stood up.

I need some fresh air, I thought. I moved from our table and made it to the next one in the direction of the bar. I immediately sat down. There was space and I could breathe. The room was dark and the music, now a dull beat, mixed in with the flashing lights of the disco dance floor glitterball.

I do not know how long I rested there before I had company again. I was sat with my head in my hands when I felt both my arms being violently pulled behind me by someone who pinned them to the rear of my chair. I instinctively looked up. Wrong move. They were back. My view of his grimacing smirk was intermittently broken by the snapping of my head from side to side as his fists smashed into my face over and over again. An eternity was shorter.

Not knowing how it came to end, probably the coward's fitness got the better of him, I slumped forward having my arms released by his accomplice. Round Two.

Why? The question repeated over and over in my brain. What had triggered this physical and later mental demoralisation in front of my friends, peers, strangers, and all those girls who would now not want anything to do with me?

No way. No more, no way. I had to get out. I looked around and unsurprisingly I had a lot of space around me now. Everyone had backed off and stared. Despite the room spinning, I could see the concern, the surprise, the shock and the pity on their faces. I read their minds. It demoralised me instantly. I was being judged for being beaten up. I had not fought back. I couldn't. I felt that I was the only one who had not seen it coming as I read the reactions of all around.

It was obvious that these large blokes had the run of the club. It was very plain to see what they were doing. No one came to help, and I couldn't see anything happening to stop it.

Pure instinct kicked in. Get out and get out now. I could not endure a third attack. The main door was somewhere in the corner of the front of the nightclub, next to the bar. Get up, walk through the crowd, get out, and get home. Simple. As I did, a couple of my mates got up and made their way to the door with me, Damian Stokes being one of them, leaving together to make sure we got out safely.

The fresh air of the dark night stung my face as the dull physical throbbing of my head kicked in, waking me from the giddy haze that enveloped my mind. I was out and on my way.

Suddenly, there was a shooting pain at the back of my head. I was on the pavement looking up at the nightclub roof. I had been punched from behind. My attempt to leave the nightclub had not gone unnoticed and I had been immediately followed. They were back and now I was on the floor trying to escape.

A taxi was parked a short distance away and my friends immediately tried to engage with the driver to take us from the scene, seemingly the only way to escape. The taxi driver was having nothing to do with it.

I felt one of these gorillas' boots kick me deep in the ribs and stomach as I tried to pick myself up onto my knees. How much worse can it get? Round Three.

That pain deep inside my body urged me to find some survival trait and forced me to get up. My mates still pleaded with the driver as Damian became the brunt of their attention. Other faces were now at the nightclub door, none of which were friendly. They were the ones who had earlier surrounded me so I could endure the first unprovoked attack without being able to fight back. I had to get up and had to get away.

With that I staggered to the taxi. The driver had no option as I opened the back door. My two mates piled in. I recalled the driver shouting "bloody hell" as he put his foot down and drove us from the sea front nightclub.

I looked back at the two males. They appeared like monsters, laughing and congratulating each other re-enacting how one had head-butted me, the other holding me whilst his accomplice pounded my face, jerking his head side to side, and then wildly kicked me to my body.

Whilst they cruelly wallowed in the victory of their cowardly act, I memorised their faces, engraining them into my memory for life. Somehow, I was going to make sure I would never endure that again, no matter what I had to do to avoid it. If it meant I never went out to another party, so be it. If that was how life treated me, then life can get lost. Not interested. Don't want it. Not going to live it.

On a lighter note, as the taxi driver dropped us a short distance away, I had the sense of checking my bodily damage. Amongst the early signs of swelling to my face and body, the pain and the anguish, I was devastated. At some stage of the attack, one of those gits had ripped my new red frilly shirt. I really was not happy.

Over time, my physical injuries came and went. The pain diminished from the swellings and bruising. However, the mental anguish was much longer. I tried to hide a lot of it as I did not want a reminder for people to ask me what had happened, and I would have to relive the incident all over again.

So that was the end of many parties for me. The thought of even being in a crowd of unknown people was frightening. Everywhere I went, I looked for those two faces and I thought I saw them no matter where I was. I had a great group of friends who would be round each other's houses most evenings and weekends, but following the incident, it was a no show from me.

The parties continued. I stayed at home. I heard through my mates who these two blokes were. I made a mental note of their names. Names that became etched in the back of my mind alongside their faces to this very day.

I have never spoken in depth of this evening to anyone for the feeling of mental reprisal in the form of anguish and humiliation. I did not want to be reminded of the shame this heaped on me for years to come. How introverted I became. How sickened at my own failure. How much I loathed being a victim and how much I venomously detested from the lowest part of my inner soul the perpetrators who chose to do this to innocent, innocuous individuals. People who by no fault of their own have their lives turned upside down and live in fear, distress and anxiousness, from which some never recover.

One day I would have my revenge and it would be something special, I promised myself.

9

A Reason to Believe

Christmas of 1981 came and went, and the winter nights were long. The small black and white portable TV in my bedroom served me well during this time since that dreadful night. My soul-searching time spent feeling safer staying indoors had allowed me to return to my love of art. When the three TV channels failed to inspire me (yes just three in those days, unless you pointed the house aerial towards the west country!) the pencils would come to life and the darkness would disappear.

I started to get more confident, drawing portraits of my heroes at the time. Rod Stewart featured a few times, David Bowie, Hazel O'Connor, Toyah, Steve Strange, Sylvester Stallone, Tom Selleck and Blondie among others.

It brought me self-satisfaction and a distraction from those inner dark moments that caused me self-doubt and fear. Art was starting to focus me and allow some escape, despite my earlier fateful interview with the Careers Advisor redirecting me towards the RAF. Perhaps I should have not said that I had once stayed on an airfield camp and liked the air show. If I had only said that I once stayed in Hay on Wye and loved its book fayre, I would now be a famous author and this book would be something totally different.

My music would be playing through my Sennheiser headphones, Bowie, Springsteen, Rod, punk, disco, heavy metal, driving me through the nights endlessly drawing, sometimes until dawn, sleeping little. School and A levels somewhere in daylight hours, an evening paper round executed in haste for the fear of those faces appearing somewhere in that outside world, and back to the sanctuary of my art, my music and my solitary confined space.

It was late January and I needed a haircut. With a couple of coins, I made my way to the local hairdressers. "The usual sir?" Alan Jones would always comment, followed closely by "Does your mother know?" referring to my very first spikey haircut he gave me some years earlier with me carrying a Rod Steward LP cover for his inspiration and swearing blind that my mother had given me permission to have such a cut.

As I had entered the hairdressers, I noticed a poster on the door advertising karate for beginners. I sat in the chair as my hair started to take shape, wondering if I could do this thing they call karate. Just think, if I could do karate, I would be able to stop anyone from attacking me again. I would be able to go out in the evenings. I could go to parties. All those people who had picked on me before would think twice. How cool would that be? I could look after my mates. I may even get a new girlfriend.

"I'm in," I said spontaneously to the voice in my head. "In what?" replied Alan Jones creating my spikey look. "Umm," I replied, realising I had inadvertently spoken aloud. "Is that your poster on the door?" I asked sheepishly. "Yes, it is," he replied. "Are you interested Ian?"

I had known Alan from the day he opened his hairdressers when I was nine years old, and my mother sat me in his booster chair (well, a small plank across the arms of the existing chair) and told him that he was to cut my hair so she didn't have to bring me back for a while. That first cut had lasted ten months.

As I went to reply, the nerves kicked in. It was not for me. It is not the thing that kids like me do or are able to be part of. My heart pounded. Why had I spoken out? But I had to. I needed to help myself some how and it was there glaring at me in the mirror's reflection, 'Beginners Starting 2nd February 1982'.

"Yes" I said with a burst of confidence. Take that my Gemini darkness. "I want to join".

And so, I did.

10

Start at the Bottom

Karate training was a strange revelation to me. It was not like any of the school activities that I had endured. It was not even like the one and only Judo lesson I took when I was eleven. I had hated every moment of it, trying to do some sideways roll being demonstrated by a big kid in white pyjamas tied with a coloured belt. I could tell that he was starting to dislike me as I was the only one of the new beginners who couldn't do what he wanted and, apparently, we were not to progress until we did this one daft wonky roll.

I was told to go in the corner and keep doing it until I could and then I would be allowed join the rest of the class. My lack of agility won that day. I never joined the others who progressed to something interesting. I hated Judo. I hated Martial Arts. They were stupid. I was never going to do them ever again. I was eleven.

Five years later and now a victim both physically and mentally, this was a must. It did not matter how hard it was going to be, it did not matter who was teaching me, I was not going to be pinned to a chair or put on the floor ever again. I had to get something out of this and not be one of life's sorry faces who everyone pitied, laughed at and eventually forgot about.

For support, I cajoled some of my mates to join as well - Stuart Warner (alias Paddy) and David Jeffcott. All three of us were excited but nervous as we clumsily commenced our very first karate lesson. Little did I know then that I would get to where I am today as one of Harada Sensei's 5th Dan Black Belts, the highest grade awarded in our organization, become a member of the Karate Do Shotokai (KDS) UK Technical Executive and still be training some thirty-eight years later. I could just about tie my belt up and stop myself from tripping over my kit bottoms.

It was not long before I had my first grading. Success, and I was off. For the first time in my life since my cycling proficiency test aged ten, I had achieved a reward for a physical activity. It was hard work using different muscles that were yet to grow, let along perform. I was used to playing football all day, only returning home at teatime when I was hungry, as instructed by my mother.

I was also used to the physical exercise of bike riding. When I was twelve years old, I had a paper round that took me and my Chopper Mark I to the very top of Penarth, down the beach front and then up the hills to the rich peoples' houses. That was a tough ride, especially in the winter when, in the snow and ice, I would lose control of my Chopper bike and end up sliding on my newspaper bag down Beach Hill with my bike following behind, shredding the bag and the South Wales Echos to boot. Try delivering the news with the sports section in tatters to rich people in Penarth. Many a time I would be told "I'll have your job boy," and being too shy to say boo to a goose, the reply that formed in my head "Get lost, you wouldn't get up the hill, you fat git!" was replaced with the word "Sorry."

I found that I just about kept up with the other budding beginners in the class, but it was my new found stubbornness that drove me on, block after block, session after session, collecting bruises, aching muscles and strained joints. Perhaps this stubbornness would eventually emerge in improved confidence to once again allow me to join friends on the teenage party social scene.

I started to travel on the occasional weekend karate course that sprung up somewhere in the UK. I recall a car or two would travel on a Sunday to a sports centre or university campus and as soon as we would arrive, we would immediately enter the fray. No warmup, just straight into battle. It was only after a while that I realized that we were actually late every time and therefore missed the warm-ups completely. No sooner had we arrived and trained like crazy demons, than we were back in the car on route to South Wales again.

It was on my very first visit to Southampton University Karate Do Shotokai that I witnessed Harada Sensei, the Principal and founder of our organization. I recall walking into the sports hall with the rest of our carload, late as usual, and I eagerly started to look around for him. I had been told that he was on this course and I would get to see the legend, the Japanese Master who introduced modern day karate to South America in the late 1950s and then into Europe in the early 1960s.

Before I knew it, we were shepherded into two lines facing an opponent each. There had to be one hundred people in the hall, all crammed shoulder to shoulder in posture waiting for a command to start. Totally focused on the threat in front of me, I soon lost any notion of looking for Sensei as the ugly giant of a Black Belt stared down at me, his fist two feet from my nose. The commands were shouted out and I lost my breath within thirty seconds. Such was the intensity of this guy's attacks that all I could do was continually move backwards out of his reach in a desperate attempt at self-preservation.

I had been training for four months and I was way out of my depth trying to defend against this reincarnated devil in a white kit and black belt. Oh my god, this was intense. Wave after wave, I could barely see the attacks, let alone move from them. No way could I possibly beat him to it, which I think was the point of this training. But that was lost in the first punch I received.

Then without realizing, my body was stepping back and fore getting closer and moving in such a way it appeared that I was goading this attacker into coming for me. I heard a faint voice but could not link it with anything I was doing, my brain was in meltdown with the noise of one hundred attackers and defenders in the hall. Something really strange was happening.

As I was frantically trying to survive, I felt my body accelerate forward with a speed that I had never experienced before. I saw my opponent's fist start to move towards me from his waist, but it never got to me. In slow motion I tried to get my fist out in time to hit him as I travelled at lightning speed into his space. I crashed straight into his chest without him being able to get his feet fixed on the floor, and he took off backwards. I tried to stop myself from falling and just regained some balance to see him on the floor in front of me sprawled and disheveled.

I felt a hand on my shoulder. I turned and heard in a Japanese accent the words, "You learn just like that." With a laugh and a finger pointing at the mountain of a black belt who wore a face of disbelief, Harada Sensei had made a point.

Harada Sensei, the main man, the one and only. Wow. I was the little spotty kid from Penarth with no self-confidence fighting a giant and, in an instant, he had maneuvered my body and taken on this titan and shown me how to win. That moment stayed with me all session, the whole trip home and even today I reflect on it and its influence on my karate and on many aspects of my life. Step forward at the right time with the right structure and confidence and even the giants in this world can be overcome.

I went on to have many further exhilarating experiences training with Harada Sensei and the instructors he has created to date, travelling throughout the UK and of course abroad and I wonder where I would be today without such guidance.

At around the same time as this fantastic experience, I earned my very first injury. To date, I have collected many broken bones, ruptured discs, torn muscles, bruised and cut skin. I have been operated on, stitched up, massaged, frozen, stretched and rehabbed to the limit. None of these injuries are talked more of by my mother than the one I received from my mate and best man Roy Margetts.

Now, Roy claims I slipped and fell onto his fist, which is partially true in some respect. I did slip to the side, but I do not know what his hand was doing so low, apart from travelling towards my right eye. It would not have been so bad, but it closed up and went black very quick. It also would not have been so bad had there not been a rather special event in a couple of days' time. If the dress code had been dark clothing, I might have got away with it. No, no chance. My mother's wedding, with me in the family photos wearing a cream jacket and white shirt, smiling away for the camera for posterity sporting the biggest and most fashionable black eye. Happy Wedding Day Mum.

11

A Step into the Unknown

After A Levels I enrolled in Portsmouth Polytechnic on a course studying Quantity Surveying. However, I had caught a bad bout of glandular fever and ended up with the option of starting all over again on that or another course or find a job. The latter seemed the correct decision.

Following a couple of jobs, I ended up working for two years in the Cooperative Bank in Cardiff and then in Caerphilly, where serving the public in a traditional valley town overlooking the castle was a fantastic experience. It taught me so much on how to interact with people from all walks of life. It was an absolute scream of a time with many stories to tell sometime in the future.

But still, there was something missing in my life. A destiny, a calling, I have no idea how to describe it. I knew I could do better. I wanted to help others, I wanted to make a difference.

For some time, I had been considering my role as a victim in this life and what it had taught me. I had great friends and a supporting family, but this act horrified me still. During this period, I had achieved the hallowed grade of Black Belt 1st Dan in karate, but I was still anxious and nervous in unfamiliar groups and especially out on the town. I still looked for those faces from that nightclub in Penarth that were etched in my mind.

Other people's perception of what my abilities were now I was a Black Belt was far greater than the confidence I took from achieving it. I was very proud to have excelled in my physical abilities and to have been awarded it, but still, there was something missing.

The bravado that my friends took from the fact that I held this new skill worried me. I still lacked the confidence of others I saw on a Saturday night, and one day I may need to defend myself or my mates in a similar situation, a notion which played heavily as a consideration when planning to go out. Having a Black Belt did not make me feel any safer.

Coming to terms with my lack of confidence was proving difficult. However, there was one overarching factor to all of this. If it was easy for me to become a victim to such abhorrent human behaviour, I would imagine that I was not the only one in this life who had been on the receiving end of such. I wanted to be able to make certain that as long as I lived, I could play my part and make sure that people were protected and prevented from becoming victims in the first place. Life was hard enough as it was without such unnecessary setbacks.

With this in mind, I took a very large step into the unknown. I joined South Wales Police.

Make or break. I was keen and enthusiastic. I was nervous and reserved. I had had my small amount of confidence taken from me in one humiliating act. I had tried to correct this by attaining a Black Belt in karate. Perhaps a career in the Police may very well serve my need and desire to put the world right and protect the innocent. But it was one hell of a move. It would most definitely either make me into something I lacked and needed to become, or it would break me and banish me to life as an eternal victim with the rest of the other poor wretched souls.

So, on a fine and sunny Monday morning on the 20th July 1987, suitcase in one hand, letter of acceptance in the other, I walked in through the gate of South Wales Police Headquarters, Bridgend. Eighteen weeks of residential training between here and the Cwmbran Police Training Centre and then out onto the streets.

By now, I realized that this was so far removed from my world of creativity, the art classroom in school, the comfort of my bedroom creating my next masterpiece, that I could not express it in words.

But that was my path, the very one that two events had guided me towards. Firstly, the advice in school to forget art as a career and find a conformist's role, regulated by structure and service. And second, a humiliating and frightening beating, stealing the little confidence I had and driving me to seek the self-preservation skills of a different kind of art, a martial art.

I now embodied a combination of them both, standing in a brand-new police uniform swearing allegiance to the Queen in front of twenty two strangers who were to be my soul saviours and colleagues. My new career had begun.

I did not excel in the classroom at all. There were some bright people there as well as very confident individuals. They could get on their feet and talk to the whole of the class. Boy, that was something. I was ok for the physical aspects but volunteering for speaking, no thanks. I receded into the background, not wanting to have my insecurity compromised by being asked a question that I could not answer or allowing embarrassment to be shown right across my face. I did not stand out at all and this was going to be a real tough test of character.

However, there was a fitness test to get through and I knew I was fit. I had scored well in the recruitment process coming top of my interview group. I started to realise that not as many people were in my fitness league. Perhaps this was a moment to shine and achieve some small moment of self-satisfaction.

Tailoring my karate exercises to the fitness test requirements had in fact been a smart move. The gym test was press-ups, sit ups and burpees, all of which were simple movements that, if broken down and concentrated on, can be performed at speed. To complete each one, relax, focus, finish, move on.

At the first test, I beat the Police Training Centre record, simple. At the second weeks later, despite again beating my own record, I was beaten by another recruit and my fitness rival. On the final occasion at the end of the whole training programme, I had the Physical Training Instructors assessing me in every minute detail to make sure that if I beat it a last time, it would be witnessed and recorded as something special. I did not let them down.

I trashed the record and set one which to this date, I have not heard of anyone surpassing or even coming close to. Try doing 127 press-ups in a minute and you will equal one part of this record. I was there, accepted and feeling more accomplished. Recognition for something different was good.

However, this training environment was not the most pleasant of experiences as were being prepared for the difficulties that we knew very little of. Apart from the physical training, I questioned whether this was the role for me more than ever.

Throughout the training, I started to create a persona to deal with this new educational process and the change that would be required to survive it. It was like an alter ego, an out-of-body experience looking at myself from the other side of the room. I could disassociate from the shy unconfident individual and apply the skills of a self-assured Police Officer, tackling problems on behalf of others. It was as if I had entered an acting career and my role now was to be this character. I was about to face the world with a great proportion of hatred and anger about to be thrown in, I needed this to work.

It took me nearly fourteen weeks to settle and feel more confident in many aspects of this environment. However, it was time for the next stage and we were shipped back to our force and churned out into the big bad world as paid servants to paper over the cracks of injustice in an ever evolving society, to play our part and make that difference to the world. Being lost in a world of colour, sketching, and creating wonderful drawings was the furthest thing from my mind. I had moved on.

The pay I now received was triple that which I had earned as a cashier in the bank. The memories of those Police Officers coming to pay in their wages every forth Thursday before an exciting weekend of night shifts, used to fill me with wonder and awe. Now I was there, by the skin of my teeth. "There is no money in art" rung in my mind. Well, there looks like there is money in crime alright. You have just got to make sure you are the one who is on the right side of it.

What followed was a probationary period on a shift at a station that I had been allocated to. This was a time when even the strongest willed can crack under the pressure and for those like me who are not confident, can be the most troublesome moment in life. I had created a character to get through training and whilst hating it, I was determined not to be beaten. The goal was too great to lose sight of and this was the next step on the road to achieving it.

I first started on the shift at Canton Police Station, Cardiff. It was a wonderful liberating experience now I was qualified enough to play a part. I could ensure that people who were different would not become victims of crime. This was in the days when a shift would consist of sixteen Police Officers in various stages in their career, a vast array of characters and experience, and of course plenty of skulduggery. Rank, officers with more experience and a pecking order ruled without question and the newest arrival being the lowest of the low to some members.

It was commonplace to ridicule the junior member of staff. So much so that as a direct result of this 'character building' process, some officers never made it through this critical probationary period and left. It was no more than full on bullying. I had learned very early that I was going to be vulnerable to this, and therefore created small behaviours that would make some of these selfish mindless morons think twice about ridiculing me.

One thing that I noticed about the group of people with these traits was that there was nothing more flawed than their own perception of others and what they did not know. Over the first few months, those that had immediately picked on me with jokes behind my back and cruel acts, realised from listening to the better officers that I was teamed up with, that I had a physical ability to deal with violence proficiently on the streets. Slowly but surely, the antics ceased as these individuals grew wary of what I was capable of doing, with their assumption that I could do something physical to them and their own fear, they stopped in the main.

Their perception of me and my karate was far greater than my confidence in myself. Come to think of it, their perception of me was far higher than my respect for them. I knew full well that my karate ability was being stretched to its limits, battling against my lack of confidence as well as the violence we faced.

However, who was I to quell any positive imagery of me that they had, that was preserving my wellbeing?

Making the tea at the start of a shift was the youngest member's responsibility and engrained into the probationary period without question. Every shift someone would moan about the standard, too hot, too cold, too strong, etc. When there were no teabags it was my fault, even though I had no responsibility for replenishing the stock. At the start of one night shift, I had had enough as all the teabags were gone and I was again going to get a load of jibes and subsequent unwanted things happen to me during the shift. I could hear voices shouting insults as I hurriedly searched for teabags.

There were none whatsoever. Apart from those at the bottom of the tall bin in the corner. Yes, those mixed with the leftover fish supper that I had cleaned from the kitchen worktop to get to the kettle the night before. In for a penny I thought as I quickly pulled these teabags mixed with the dog food chunks from feeding the stray mongrel caged in the rear yard, the chicken curry trays of the afternoon shift and of course the fish supper.

Tea was served as the abusive comments for its late arrival diminished. I sat and watched as gradually one by one, those that had ridiculed me greedily snatched at the pot to pour tea for the Sergeant and for themselves before others. They started to drink it. Their looks of contentment gradually changing to bewilderment as they inwardly queried what they were tasting, but nevertheless continued to drink. The first call of the night came over the radio and as the junior person, I acknowledged it. I got up to attend whilst the bewildered looks turned to screwed up faces of disgust with two of the worst bullies making exceptionally good impressions of cats regurgitating fur balls.

The cursing hit the roof as I left the station laughing to myself. The internal investigation carried on all night, coming to the conclusion that someone had swapped our teabags for some of those fancy healthy cleansing fruit flavoured ones. Yes, those dog-food-chicken-tikka-mackerel-fruit-flavoured ones!

One of the Sergeants on my shift was in the habit of turning a blind eye to the bullying and occasionally joined to be part of the in crowd. So it was with some inner satisfaction that, many years later, I walked into a valleys police station as the newly promoted Inspector to find one of my Sergeants who I now supervised in the cell complex in my new role, looking back at me with a confused expression. The very same Sergeant who allowed such bullying all those years ago was about to be supervised by the victim of his poor supervision and antiquated regime. Yes, me.

It is a small world indeed and what goes around comes around, and as I realised once more, how you treat people will always come back to you eventually. In this case, the retribution came when I realised that the Sergeant would awkwardly try to steer clear of conversations of the old shift some sixteen years previous. He knew of his misgivings and that was enough for me. In return, I made sure that I was the most professional Inspector this person could have asked for. And the first thing I would do when I would walk into the cell complex, would be to make him a cup of tea.

12

A Return to the National Assembly for Wales

For a decade I was the Police Inspector in charge of the Police Unit at the National Assembly for Wales. A gem of a role in the policing world, which was treated with contempt by a few and jealousy by others. Little did people know the intrigue of such a position or even consider the nature of contact with prominent politicians and business driven leaders.

Considering most Police Inspectors would be moved around to another department or station after three years on average, I lasted ten years in the same position at the Assembly. I must have given the impression that I knew what I was doing, had friends in high places, or I had been totally forgotten about. I would like to think that it was the first, but I know the role carried a load of grief and was not for those who put themselves and their careers before everything else. Politicians were not to be crossed. Their contacts and influence were far reaching, and you needed to ensure that everything you did was justified and fitted their agenda without fail.

At times, you dealt with their issues in the strictest of confidence which meant you spoke to no one about it. No one whatsoever. It was enough to make many a Senior Police Officer visiting the Unit to try and make their mark and change our working system, run for their lives when I would relay a 'hypothetical' scenario for their consideration. "As long as you have such a matter in hand, Ian, if it was ever to occur, there is no need to involve me," they would say, recalling an urgent meeting they needed to get to elsewhere, grabbing their paperwork and hat, scurrying away not to be seen for a further six months or more.

When the National Assembly first opened and I arrived as a Police Constable in 1999, I watched this Inspector role develop. The whole environment intrigued me. It was a total hotbed of civil servants controlling politicians controlling civil servants. The first steps of independence, the chaos versus the conformity, with police, press and anarchists thrown into the mix, made for a totally different approach to dealing with conflict and problem solving.

However, having come from years of shift work, which is probably the worst thing about modern-day policing, I found myself on day shifts, sleeping well and feeling refreshed for the first time in a while. As a result, I felt like a new challenge and rekindled my wish to become promoted. I had passed my promotion exams some years before but had not really paid much attention to passing the interview scenarios. Now. with the energy and time, I gave it one more try. I passed and within six months of arriving, I was off. That was not expected.

As a newly promoted Sergeant back on the streets, managing a shift and again running myself into the ground working all hours, I yearned for that day when I would be able to return to the Assembly Unit when the current Sergeant was moved on. However, it dawned on me that this may not happen as my old Sergeant looked determined to stay. It was a devastating moment of truth when the penny dropped. In order to return, I would have to apply myself to a new set of examinations, assessments and interviews to be further promoted to Inspector and return to the National Assembly for Wales higher up the food chain.

Therefore, as had happened in many other aspects of my life, this became the number one plan. To get promoted again and seek the skills necessary to jump the hurdles and through the hoops and be the number one candidate for this position when the opportunity arrived.

Promoted again, the current Unit Inspector carried on working in his post for a further three years. During this period, I was given the onerous role of running the cell complexes spread around the valleys of South Wales, by far the worst job I'd come across. I never knew who caused me more heartache in that role, the prisoners, the solicitors, or the staff employed to look after these so-called clients.

It would not be uncommon for me to arrive at one of the police stations at 6:45 am on a Monday morning to a queue of nightshift staff workers waiting in line to complain to me about other Police Officers, incidents and the general downfall of their lives over the previous weekend. I would enter the building to face a list of detainees who wanted to complain about their treatment, and I would continue all day and all week receiving complaints about everything. As soon as I put one fire out, another one started. I should have been in the Fire Service.

I was privileged enough to have an office away from the cell complex. That is of course, if you call a converted drunk cell directly opposite the booking in area a privilege. The ridiculously small confined space did actually have some light, albeit to look out of the window, I would have to stand on the desk and hold onto the bars just in case I slipped.

Fortunately, following a refurbishment, the organisation did actually allow me to replace the cell gate with an actual door which I thought was very considerate of them. However, during the hot summer months, I was continually reminded of the history of that cell with a toxic aroma of bleach partially masking the urine wafting occasionally around the room as the heat rose in my luxury executive office suite.

However, in time, the inevitable happened. A phone call was made, and I was summoned to attend the outgoing Assembly Inspector's leaving do. I was re-introduced to the one and only Lord Dafydd Elis-Thomas who incidentally had attended my own leaving do when I was promoted from the unit some six years previously. All my hard work and years of preparation will come to the forefront that evening.

There in the corner of a Cardiff Docklands pub, surrounded by inebriated Assembly executives, politicians, a retiring Police Inspector and potential future staff, I sat opposite Lord Dafydd Elis-Thomas, the most senior politician in Wales and the Presiding Officer of the National Assembly for Wales who now acted as the chair of the impromptu delegation. This group had been ushered together to carry out the most important activity known to such public organisations, the unofficial vetting and interview of the potential candidate.

Of course, it is well known that such procedures are fictitious, and I must add do not really take place. They never have and never will. But I had waited three years since promotion to Inspector, biding my time in the godforsaken land of the cell complexes of the South Wales valleys. This was my opportunity in the back room of a seedy Cardiff Docklands pub face-to-face with the hierarchy of the Welsh political scene, my future in-hand. You must be in it to win it, and I was very much in this game to win outright.

Six weeks later, I took up my role as the Police Inspector of the National Assembly for Wales Police Unit. I had no intention of getting promoted again as that meant exposing my weaknesses of confidence and addressing groups once more. Not for me, I know my limits. I hung up my uniform, bought a new suit and set about entwining myself into the very fabric of this captivating world.

I loved the job. I had seen the potential and realised that I could really fit in with this world of intrigue, cloak and dagger, scandal and chaos. It was about being present but not being seen, making problems go away and getting the politicians around the country safe and well, and managing a great bunch of staff who enjoyed working there also. Easy, so I thought.

Caught on camera by a national newspaper as I oversee the policing operation with the Queen and members of the Royal Family attending the opening of the 3rd Welsh Assembly in June 2007

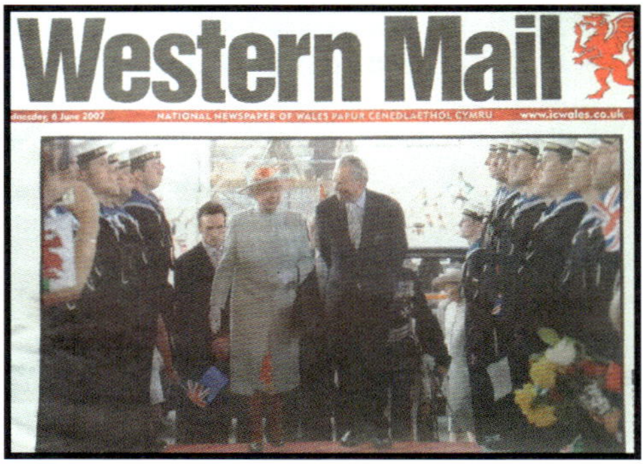

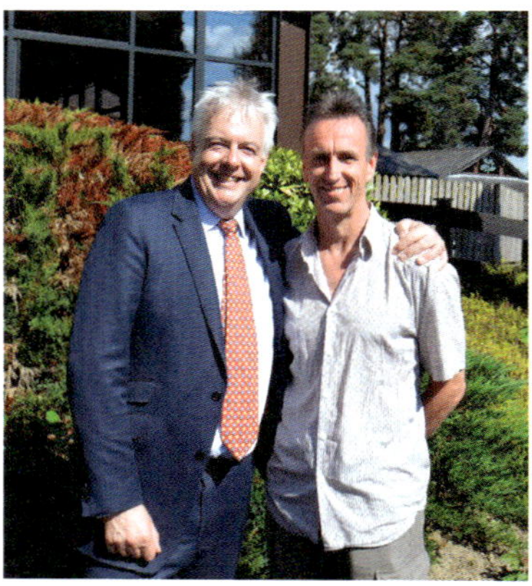

My last duty with First Minister Carwyn Jones

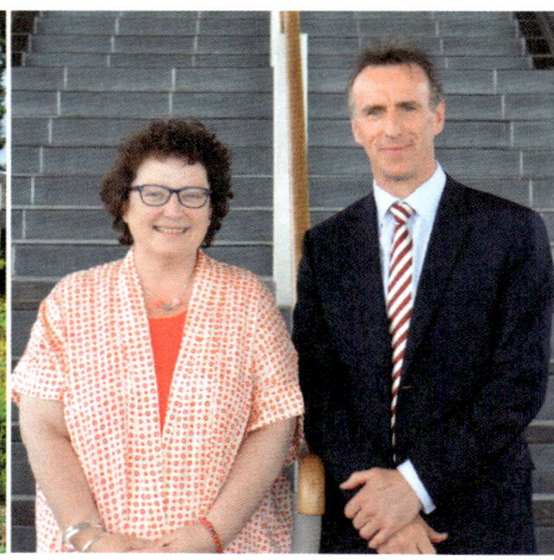

Me with Presiding Officer Elin Jones

Part Four

Born to Run

13

Political, Violent and Controversial

In considering what it was that actually brought me back to painting after all those years, I suppose I realized that my injuries from karate were not getting any easier to handle. However, years of determination to turn negative into positive to cope with my lack of confidence, ensured physical pain was a minor deterrent as I kept training to the maximum.

Karate had given me a level of confidence that had allowed me to take the step and join the Police Service and assist in keeping my shyness at bay. It had helped to keep me safe each day by testing my awareness and reactions with every person I met. I was able to read people's body language and act accordingly. I was also very aware of my own body condition and learned to control those fight or flight moments when I faced violence alone many times. It was equal respect for both the violent position I was in and the skills that I was trying to perfect that helped develop me as a person.

The stress of the danger and the need to do something using my skills greatly increased my confidence in those situations. I still loathed standing up in front of a class with a flip chart on a work training day explaining my group's activity. Give me a violent crowd over that anytime.

Knowing that around the corner was the opportunity to return to the National Assembly for Wales reassured me that I was on track with my profession and swayed me towards my old passion and a renewed drive to return to painting. What I was unaware of was the influence that my profession and this political world would have on my creative art.

So, there I was, now a Police Inspector back at the home of Welsh politics with a huge eclectic mix of life experiences that not many can claim to have been exposed to, coupled with the grandeur of politicians, journalists, TV, celebrities and anarchists. It was time to see how this intricate world worked and what it entailed.

The infighting amused me as I would sit and watch the First Minister being questioned by other Welsh political leaders. I would set up policing operations and accompany the First Minister and many of his Cabinet members around the whole of Wales, listening to their negotiations, the reasoning for their political strategy and of course watching the occasional hole that some of them dug, sometimes voluntarily jumping into it as well. Working with their support staff and various government and parliamentary departments, I can honestly say that programmes such as Yes Minister, Veep and The Thick of It, are so very true, I could swear I was in an episode of one. Perhaps for another time, maybe.

The mixing of our Police Unit within the parliamentary estate was intriguing. Whole departments were very cautious of us and our activity. The lack of trust was comical, as they truly believed we were the spies within. No one had told them that we did not care for their political policies or the spin they had just invented to negate some fact that required to be turned into fiction before others believed it. All we cared about was that they behaved themselves and did not cause us problems.

In time, these cautious departments were won over one by one. I even had the republicans seeking personal guidance and help many times when they saw the value in trusting me and my colleagues. Being seen to seek this help publicly, however, was another matter for them. Afterall, we represented the establishment and they did not. Thankfully, for the whole ten years at the Assembly, I never wore a uniform and was not recognized by some as 'the establishment'. I was there in the background, inconspicuous, watching, cajoling, and thinking about my art.

My experiences in the police had taken me from simple street crime, drunkenness, sex offenders, drugs, murders, car chases, arsons, armed criminals, large scale disorder, corruption, to counter-terrorism, anarchists, politicians, Royalty, Heads of State and confidential issues that would give some people nightmares for weeks.

It was safe to say, I had enough to invigorate even my small mind and create artwork that would be different. Therefore, it was time to move away from the scenic views I had been painting. My desire to tell stories was now stronger than ever. The stories of people and their situations, who they were and what they did and thought. My stories of them and their stories of others, how the world saw them and how they in turn saw the world. My environment was perfect. Political, violent and controversial.

14

Qualifications

One dilemma I had was whether to seek further qualifications in art. Afterall, the more qualified you are, the more experienced you appear. I had an O Level and therefore no real experience to brag of. I took some night school classes in Howard Gardens, Cardiff, the home of Cardiff University Art Department to see if this was my route. Under the guidance of Sarah Richards, I commenced what was to be an enjoyable experience.

We would meet on a Monday evening, an eclectic mix of individuals seeking solace in paint. I recall on my very first evening, having carried my Halfords toolbox full of paints, pencils, turps, mixing pots and palette into the classroom, I followed the other budding apprentices and chose an easel at the rear from which to create my masterpiece on my very first night.

I said hello to the person who had joined me and looked over to what appeared to be a person of authority starting to talk at the front of the classroom. It was Sarah Richards. A task had begun and before I knew it, we were off, with paper being passed from the front back to us. I stepped forward and reached out to take it. In doing so, I caught the lid of my Halfords toolbox which subsequently flipped open and launched all the contents of my painting equipment at the row in front. This included a half open jar of turps to add liquid to the volley.

My first 'impression' was not that associated with the famous art style, but nevertheless I did make a mark on my very first lesson in 25 years away from the art classroom.

I came to realise that it was not necessarily the attaining of qualifications that would make me a better artist, but one of watching and learning from as many people and experiences as I could. No matter what they were, if there was a tenuous link to art, I would absorb it as much as possible. The practice of being with artists and friends with the same positive attitude and interests is second to none and can be as rich, if not better than any course.

I recall discussing art in depth with Sergeant Ian Roderick on the steps of the Senedd, and whether I should seek a mentor, crying with laughter as he displayed a picture that had gone viral on social media of the somewhat tragic but comically restored nineteenth century image of Jesus Christ by local woman Cecilia Gimenez. He said, "do you think you could do better?"

I recall trips I made and continue to make to London, with a friend and fellow artist Gareth Hughes, a leading journalist in Welsh politics who has interviewed many Prime Ministers in his time. We would visit numerous galleries, the Tate Modern, Tate Britain and the Coultard Gallery to name a few, his choice of venues broadening my art experience and his pleasant conversation expanding my political knowledge.

Qualifications got you places, but experiences and practice gave you the zest for life.

15
Creativity

Perhaps I am more fortunate than others when it comes to creativity as, firstly, I am able to draw. Secondly, due to my personal experiences, I have learned to turn negative into positive and therefore become creative in a whole host of areas when needed.

However, I do believe that being creative is inside everyone, you do not have to have an artistic flare or talent to be creative. There are many occasions in life where people have been in predicaments and have had to dig deep and think differently to get themselves out of a difficult situation, from trying to feed a family on a tight budget and coming up with different options to satisfy your children, to repairing a broken household appliance until it can be mended or replaced. It is not solely owned by those who are fortunate enough to have an artistic flare. I know several people who are fantastic artists, but they cannot create original images or even come up with ideas for new artwork.

I have had to be creative to get by at times, nothing to do with art. When I was six years old in Victoria Junior School, a kid a year older than me kept wanting to be my friend at breaktime. Naively, I thought he was being nice. It turned out that I was going to be a victim of his bullying as he ramped up his nastiness and started to find me on my own, picking on me and pushing me around.

Realising this, I had to make sure I was in the middle of other kids and there was no way he could single me out each break. I devised a game based on my love of the cowboy TV programmes and sowed the seed in my mate's minds before we left the classroom each break. We all went out as a posse and whilst I took an active part in the middle, this bully had no way of getting to me. I was being creative to save my skin.

Throughout school, my shyness and lack of confidence did not encourage me to ask the questions to inform my inquisitive and creative mind. As a young person there was no internet and very few reference books that would set you on your way. However, the public library was a great source of information. There was so much, in fact, that in seeking an answer I would forget the reason why I was there and end up lost in a totally different subject.

The 1970s educational system didn't helped either. The rigorous enforcement of being sat in rows reciting multiple times tables, being given questions and then told the answers in copycat form fact after fact, didn't do much for the early thought process that existed in my very first years of school. We did not need to think, just follow, conform and repeat.

With art being an exception to this rule, we became the very products of Pink Floyds 1979 'Another Brick in the Wall Part 2' anthem, the period of classroom rows, conformity and learning set answers to given questions. At the very least, I guess, creativity was being moulded and directed to produce what was needed by society. But how many times did you ask a question to be told the answer "Because"?

The bricks were being stock-piled and constructed around our creativity as we rigidly moved through the all-important O Level syllabus. And brick by brick, we became that wall.

Being different from the mainstream certainly has its positives. One of these is that you look or act different because you think differently. This is the biggest advantage that you could ever possibly have and one that should never hold you back. Applying this to an activity, a job or a role, is ideal and people should never be convinced otherwise.

In my experience, I ended up with a fantastic group of quirky friends who for many reasons filled my life with excitement and unexpected laughter. To date, when I am struggling with creativity, I will turn to people with such traits and pick their brains on a subject or perhaps naming a painting for instance. It is not long before I have their feelings and ideas added into the mix and I am off again. I have never underestimated the thoughts of the most inconspicuous of people who I know, may and quite often do hold the gem to my next masterpiece.

Creativity comes from everywhere. People ask me where I get such ideas from and in the forthcoming chapters, I refer to specific thoughts, situations and experiences that have resulted in paintings. But you only have to look at the world around. Currently, I am embroiled in a series of paintings concerning the chaos of politics, police and society. My experiences come into play, but so do the media news flashes, the press stories and the general feeling in society right now.

However, if you just click on the internet, there are millions of images that can spark an idea for a drawing or painting. Type in a word or topic and you are off. Some of the best combinations of colours come from adverts in magazines. So much so that when I come across a fantastic picture, such as a bottle of alcohol set on a table in a bar, and the rich browns and golds make it stand out, I rip that page out for reference in the future.

I always carry a piece of paper with me and a pen and as images or words flash before me, I record them straight away. At home, I keep a pad by the bed as some of the best ideas I have had have been in the middle of the night. If I wait until morning, it is gone. Mind you, I have woken to read a note and wondered what the hell I was thinking.

I keep a journal of all the ideas that I have. Some of these have resulted in satisfying artwork to date, and some are listed for future projects when the 36 hour day gets invented which will give me more time to paint.

Creativity is yours. It is your experiences. It is what you see and what you think. You do not have to be the greatest painter to be creative. You do not have to even be that good. It is a matter of picking up a pencil, pen, brush and placing it on a surface and going with the flow. I was recently told that you cannot sit and motivate yourself to do something. You have to get up and move in that direction which will make the motivation happen.

Like life itself, it is not what happens to you, but what you are going to do about what happens to you that will make you a stronger person. With art it is not the ideas you have, it is what you are going to do with them that will make you an artist.

Music has and still is a fantastic tool for generating creativity. Just think of all those brilliant songs that you automatically tap your finger along with or quietly sing to. At times, there is nothing better than to crank up the volume and let that fast beat drive you through the start of a new piece of artwork. When it comes to detail, the slower melodic tunes set the rhythm and calm detailed imagery appears.

Going to gigs and listening to music play a huge part in my artwork. There is nothing like that atmosphere of a live concert of one of your favourite acts singing a memorable song which results in an idea, and again you reach for your phone or pen and paper. I have been invigorated many times by a song title, the lyrics or a tune, and have used such to influence an idea for a painting. Even one particular Stereophonics stage backdrop gave me the idea that I was missing for a detailed painting which appears later in this book.

Some years ago, I recall sitting on the grassy bank of the school playground next to another father and friend, both of us waiting for our five year old offspring to burst into the sun-light with their stories of today's exciting lessons.

Martyn Joseph, singer, song writer and all-round pleasant conversationalist would sit and listen as I relayed last night's shift on the streets of Cardiff Bay. The trouble, the strife, poverty stricken families entwined in the criminal fabric of the social system, locked in a perpetual downward spiral with little way out, he would ask questions of these incidents, the processes and what had happened to a particular character. He would comment that there was a lyric or a song in there somewhere, and I would wonder if any did make it onto a song sheet.

He had a number of fantastic songs which I could recognise in terms of locations and family members. A lot I did not as his travels took him to far flung places where the troubles of individuals and groups were no more to me than the media chose to place on TV. On stage he became the story telling singer, reminding us that the world had troubles no matter where. As he confesses at each gig, most of his songs are miserable, and he again is going to sing another downtrodden influenced song to cheer us all up.

Today, I wonder if his songs and his story telling lyrics influenced me back then, and made me question myself as I now try and step forward and tell stories through my art. Yes, I think he did.

I now need to paint with the same meaning as the lyrical content of Kelly Jones' song writing prowess, to create artwork with the fortitude and determination of a Bruce Springsteen or Martyn Joseph song, to capture the soulful gritty sound of Rod Stewart, and establish an adventure worthy of a Wilbur Smith novel.

That is my ultimate aim in creativity.

16

The 365 Day Challenge

There comes a time when if you want something, you just have to go for it and trust your desire to make whatever it is happen for you. Easier said than done, especially if you are as cautious as me. I mean, you are talking about the guy who before bed checks the back door to make sure that when he checked it earlier, he was right and it was locked, despite being locked earlier that evening and a family member had checked it just before.

But when you do let loose and find the ability to just go for something, it is the most brilliant, adrenaline-filled journey that you can imagine. Especially if there is an end goal that you absolutely desire.

One of my most daring moments of spontaneity came in June 2018. It was following a load of negativity surrounding my progress in art. I had spent no end of enthusiasm helping others through my 30-year career, and now it was time to transfer that effort and commitment towards my artistic talent, and make something of it for me and my family.

I got so annoyed with the cynics and doubters not believing that I could actually do it, that I committed myself one hundred percent to art. I filmed myself stating that I was going to give myself a full year to make it as an artist, and I asked everyone to come on my journey with me, even though as I said it, I didn't know where it would take me. But I was going to do it come hell or high water.

It took a while to make sure I fitted everything I wanted to say into the video in the required 58 seconds that Instagram allowed. My son Connor advised me on the best of the two clips I took and enthusiastically and with belief in me, told me to go for it. Just after 6pm on a Friday evening, I launched it on my Facebook and Instagram pages.

My wife Tracy came home from shopping and I gleefully announced what I had done.

"What do you want to do that for?" was the first remark. "Well, who else is going to promote my art for me?" I immediately replied as she continued watching the full video clip that my son was playing.

"It's a bit daft," she said. My heart sunk. That dull feeling in the pit of your stomach that would creep up on you and dictate to you, reminding you that you are trying to be someone that you can't be and never will, was back. I turned away despondently and thought I have gone and made myself look a fool, another laughingstock. It was too late; the video was out there for all to see.

We had arranged to go to the cinema within the next hour, which partially took my mind off the brief feeling of elation created by spontaneity and the following self-humiliating reality check of where I actually stood in life. I could not recall what the film was that evening, which I guess proved testament to how down I felt, having had the nerve to do something spontaneous, challenge myself and to tell the world I am on a journey and to come with me as my story develops.

In leaving the cinema complex, Connor told me to check how the post had done. I dubiously checked Facebook. I scrolled through the various posts and homed in on the video. There, below the entry were the statistics with evidence of my foolhardiness and impending embarrassment. I looked to the 'people reached' number as this would give an indication of how far the video had gone. To my amazement, in the short three hours of being away from the phone, the video had reached over one thousand people.

Connor looked at me and started to laugh. I laughed too. Oh my god, over one thousand people in three hours had been given access to the video and look at the comments as well. All positive, all helpful. My wife listened in. No comment.

This successful reach went on the next day with every check reinforcing the reason why I did the video in the first instance. The weekend came to an end and a final check on Monday evening confirmed my belief and far outreached any expectation I had as a shy, unassuming background member of this life I led. In one weekend, ten thousand people had been reached. My message was out there.

I was now really going to have to make it as an artist come what may. I had now more people watching and following than ever before. That brought worry and self-doubt, but the positive vibe I felt from everyone, far outweighed my fears. I now had people with me on my journey. There was definitely now no Plan B.

17

The Non-Famous Artist

With the changing algorithms on Facebook, certain posts were not being seen by most of my followers. In order to reach more people, I had to change tact. When I bumped into people socially, some were kind enough to ask about my artwork and my new journey in life. However, a lot of my artwork was not getting out to the people I wanted to reach.

What I need, I thought, is a publicity agent. That is it. This business of self-promotion was just not me. How could I stand up and sing the virtues of my artwork? To date, being in the public eye had been painful. Whether giving evidence in court, addressing a meeting or managing a large crowd, I was always aware that there were plenty of people watching who knew who you were and had opinions of what they believed you stood for. Sometimes they would act on those to your personal detriment, like the time I stood up and told a load of Manchester City fans whose team were losing to stop pulling a fence down and I had a dart, a golf ball and a load of coins thrown at me. Yes, I was more suited to being in the background, minding my own business and creating artwork.

A close friend of mine, Hywel Phillips, who I had worked with for several years, was known for his brazen attitude towards life. There was always something happening when he was around, and if there wasn't, he would make it. He is the only person I know who will come up smelling of roses every single time.

One afternoon, I was sat at home when my phone rang. It was Hywel. He was away for a few days and he was stood just down the road from an art gallery in Totnes, Devon. He asked me one simple question, "Do they know you in this gallery, Ian?"

I said that I doubted it very much, to which he replied "Well, they are about to" and he hung up. Knowing his devilment, I wondered what he was going to get up to. A short while later, my phone pinged and there was a video.

He had filmed himself walking into the Yvonne Coomber Contemporary Gallery, opening the door and in a forthright manner saying to the person behind the desk "Do you have any art by the famous artist Ian Mackenzie?"

The woman replied "Afraid not" shaking her head just as forthright as the filming enquirer.

"Have you ever heard of him?" he asked.

Firmly she replied, "No".

"Ok. Thanks very much," Hywel said as he reversed out of the door, capturing the woman's smile on camera which said it all.

I can't believe it, I whispered, playing it over and over again giggling to myself. That is it. I have found a marketing campaign. I was about to become famous for not being famous.

Of course, this was just the green light for Hywel to use his best entrepreneurial talent. No sooner had I posted this video on social media, he sent me another. This time it was a gallery called Trinity House Paintings in the Cotswolds.

The question was posed to the gallery assistant "Have you heard of the famous oil artist Ian Mackenzie?"

Her reply surprisingly, "No, I've never heard of him". The hunt was on. Someone somewhere must know of this artist.

He travelled abroad in his plight, firstly to the art quarter in Barcelona where he questioned street and market artists, filming them and posting their bemused looks of surprise. He asked bar staff at a restaurant, sending me their reply. I hilariously posted this stream of videos on my social media accounts, and it hit a cord with people coming up to me asking how my non-fame was progressing.

Meanwhile, other videos were being made and sent to me. Genevieve Thueux queried Amazon's Alexa, the font of all knowledge. Alexa when asked, knew nothing of me. Ioana Isac asked Siri, Apple's artificial intelligence brain, if it had anything listed on me. Everything was listed except my artwork.

Hywel visited the Galeri d'Art in the Centre Culturel of Les Carroz d'Araches in the French Alps, where filming himself talking in his best French comedy accent about his search for artwork by the famous non-famous artist Ian Mackenzie, he entered the gallery. Like a scene out of "Allo Allo", he approached a member of staff and proceeded to question her. Again, he met with another look of bewilderment.

He returned home empty handed, but that did not discourage him whatsoever. He traced and met a Welsh artist by the name of David Davis and quizzed him in his one-man plight to find if anyone had heard of the non-famous artist. His conclusion was stark.

However, as luck would have it, he next contacted me from outside The Cric Gallery in Crickhowell, Powys, Wales. This is the gallery that I had submitted the Gareth Bale painting called "Y Ddraig Rhuodd -The Dragon Roared" to, which I have featured in a chapter all of its own. It was also the gallery that I had exhibited work at previously in their open shows, one of which just weeks earlier. I knew that I had been one of over fifty artists chosen, so there was a fair chance of the staff not recalling my name. Coupled with the fact that the staff were voluntary, I was pretty sure that he would have no chance of finding someone there who would have heard of me. Oh, the irony of it all.

So, armed with his camera and his charm, once more he entered a gallery. And once more, the member of staff had no idea who I was. It was great publicity.

Enthused by his discovery that no one had heard of me, he set off to London with his son Tomos, who by now had been enlisted as the official cameraman. On a whistle stop tour, they hit the streets like a fly on the wall documentary team, recording the story leading up to that very first moment of discovery.

Early evening and Chinatown was filled with a bellowing voice asking random passersby if they had heard of the famous artist Ian Mackenzie. A restaurant promoter dressed in a full body panda suit was interrogated as to his knowledge of this Welsh artist. A romantic couple walking by, taking in the atmosphere of the evening, became victims of his questioning. No one was safe. They were on a mission.

The following day it was the turn of the Halcyon Gallery, New Bond Street, Mayfair. This is probably the most luxurious and spectacular gallery that I have visited to date and it was about to be descended upon by the non-famous artist seeking film crew. If this went terribly wrong, my dream of one day exhibiting there could very easily become my nightmare, and I may very well become the first named artist to be barred from frequenting the gallery ever again, let alone hanging a piece of artwork. On the plus side, they do say that publicity is publicity.

In they went, camera secretly rolling. A search of exhibited artwork proved fruitless. There were no Ian Mackenzie's to be found. Hywel turned to staff and engaged them with his quest to see if they had any work by the non-famous artist. Bewilderment ensued. He mentioned the subject matter. Still no recognition. So, he changed tact and enquired about the non-famous artists' favourite influential painter to date, Mitch Griffiths. A lightbulb went on with the curator and off they went downstairs to be educated in all things arty.

No Ian Mackenzie's, no knowledge whatsoever, but the very first introduction to the Halcyon Gallery, and my name mentioned in the same breath as Mitch Griffiths which cannot be a bad start in publicity terms.

My position in the artworld seemed to be emerging. If I were going to make it in the art world, I would probably make it as a famous artist who became known for not being famous.

Part Five

Every Picture Tells a Story

18

Cenedl o Obaith - Nation of Hope

In travelling around Wales, visiting art galleries in the four corners of the principality, I was always in awe of the paintings they displayed. I would quickly nip into these local businesses and absorb as much information as I could in a short time, and then spend endless hours trying to understand the techniques that artists used to capture such landscapes and scenes. The beaches, the countryside, and the animals of Wales were all caught on canvas in various styles and materials.

However, there always seemed that something was missing. Everywhere I went, I saw cottages of various shapes and sizes, fields of sheep and the occasional farmer, all painted very nicely framed and waiting for that red dot that sits alongside a successful sale. Occasionally, I would see a small collection of figures or something that was different, but in the main, there appeared a level of conservatism in the choice of art displayed by the galleries which in turn fed the demand of the customer.

This was a little perplexing to me, as although I appreciate the skills of painting this type of artwork, and knowing artists who produced such work, I have to take my hat off to them, they are seeing something in landscapes that at best fails me most times. But I guess that is the joy of art. Everyone is able to make a choice about what they like and what they create.

I had been making steady progress with different mediums, surfaces, equipment and styles and had painted a number of canvases, some good, some terrible, looking to see where I fitted in to this vast world of art. However, I figured oil was my choice, as I had a desire to create artwork like the masters such as Caravaggio and Salvador Dali.

By now I had visited many galleries outside of Wales and had seen a vastly different collection of artwork compared to that of Welsh galleries. One gallery in particular had impressed me, and one certain artist stood out from all the rest by a mile. I had seen a Sunday newspaper supplement with a painting of the English actor Ray Winstone draped in the Union Jack flag. The detail and look were amazing. Within two days I had taken leave and I travelled to London to see this painting in person.

I walked into the Halcyon Gallery in New Bond Street, Ian Mackenzie, a complete nobody from the land that time forgot, and my jaw dropped. Painting after painting hung on every wall, and they were anything but small. These were life size, each one a character telling a story itself of a social, economic, or human situation. I could not believe the quality.

After two hours of absorbing every piece of artwork, a member of staff approached me. She said that she had been watching me, seeing my keenness in the exhibition, and queried if I had yet viewed the main piece, referring to the Ray Winstone portrait. I had not, I replied.

She then led me into a private part of the gallery separated from the rest and there it was. The most stunning painting I had ever seen. I stared at it without blinking for what seemed an eternity. The look, the content, even the colours told the story. This was on a totally new level to anything I had ever seen before. I was blown away.

Sometime later, as I pulled myself together and came back in to reality, the same member of staff kindly handed me the show brochure, which I thanked her for and for her kindness in allowing me to see all the paintings in the collection.

Without any further delay, I hurried to Paddington train station to get back to Wales as soon as I could. I had seen my future. There was no more confusion of what to paint. It was absolutely clear. People told stories, art told stories and I was going to paint people who in turn would tell the stories I wanted to tell.

Sat on the train, I opened the art show book. It was titled "The Promised Land," the artist a person by the name of Mitch Griffiths. I had a new hero to follow.

It took a while to gain the confidence to start painting people seriously. I had been creating landscapes of late, and people were a whole new concept. However, this was my path and this path was one that I was choosing, not anyone else, so I needed to find a way to succeed.

I practiced copying images from the internet and magazines, but I needed to paint what I termed as real people. Again, my confidence prevented me from stepping forward and asking people who I thought would be great characters to capture. But if I wanted to succeed, I would have to ask them, and my desire was now greater than my fear. Perhaps the balance mentally was being forced to finally tip in my favour.

One or two people were not interested, I guess it was not for them, but others were extremely helpful, especially those who knew me quite well. Giulia Bergamin, Sioned Lewis, Gareth Hughes and Sonam Griffiths from various offices within the Assembly estate were soon captured in oil on canvas, with Giulias portraits exhibited in the corridors of the Assembly itself. In her role managing visits by foreign diplomats, many of her organized tours passed her portraits. This caused a few inquisitive questions and hurriedly translated answers, as, much to the tours' amusement, I had portrayed her as representing two of the Seven Deadly Sins.

As I experimented, my son Connor became my main subject that I practiced photographing and painting. He was developing his love for guitar playing, and therefore was a great character to work with. Later, members of the Police Unit became my focus in various forms as well as leading Welsh politicians, offering their services upon quest.

I was very fortunate to be in a position where I was now experiencing the working lives of the movers and shakers in our society, the powerhouse of the Welsh economy and the troubles that come with this arena. My ideas for paintings started to turn towards this new dimension.

A path from youthful experiences to the impact of Mitch Griffiths and my position within the political amphitheater, was definitely now stirring a deep-seated emotion within me. It was time to start to create artwork that truly reflected me, my unbridled passion, enthusiasm, and desire for something.

I had an idea. I wanted to create a painting that represented Wales. I wanted it to say more than just the cottages and scenes that other artists had successfully portrayed over the years. I wanted it to be powerful and memorable and stand out as a strong independent image of a country that for many years had been in the shadow of the other British nations. It had to be different and it had to say something modern for it to be remembered.

For some time, I had worked for and alongside organizations that were bucking the trend of the stereotypical male leadership that continues to dominate society. Both South Wales Police and the National Assembly for Wales in Cardiff

Bay were headed by females, with Barbara Wilding (QPM) and Dame Claire Clancy holding the respective posts. Furthermore, a political move within the National Assembly saw Lord Dafydd Elis-Thomas succeeded by Dame Rosemary Butler as the Presiding Officer, who when stood down, was replaced by Elin Jones AM. This completed the trio of positions in Wales all held by women, who I was ultimately accountable to at various times over the last ten years of my police career.

There could not be many more forward-thinking nations in terms of equality or ones that had successful women holding the top positions for law enforcement, parliamentary and political establishments.

That was it. It was as plain as daylight. A small nation downtrodden, who throughout history was dominated by the sheer size and power of their neighbours. A hard working populous with its history entrenched in coal mining, the toughest of physical labour creating the wealth of the nation, which was shipped out of Cardiff Bay, the busiest port in the world. The fictitious dragon emblazoned across the nations flag, portraying defiance, and the fight within. The spirit of never giving up, regardless of anything. And the progressive transformation of embracing cultural change and modernism, celebrating the role of women as equals.

I needed someone who would capture this and be the essence of a modern image that was vital. There were many celebrities that came to mind, both male and female. But of course, getting access to them would be a minefield to navigate, and maybe the image that I wanted to create would be lost on the fact that the celebrity may become the focal point rather than the story itself.

So, to find the right person was the next plan. I was extremely fortunate working within the Assembly estate in the Bay, and in particular in my role there, as I had access to all the restricted offices throughout. I wore a suit most days and I could freely move and speak with people and departments confidentially and without fuss. Of course, holding my rank, I was quite sought after at times to assist with many dilemmas that staff and politicians found themselves in, each with a further story to tell in time perhaps.

The Welsh Government occupied the top floor of one of the Assembly buildings, and I was forever dealing with Ministerial diaries, checking their movements, advising on their security and putting confidential plans in place to ensure their safety around the principality. In doing so, I got to know a young lady who I can only describe as the embodiment of my next art project. Her feistiness, her charm and her vulnerability all wrapped in the Welsh flag, epitomized the strong Welsh image that I wanted to capture.

She had the character and stood for the normal everyday hard-working member of our nation. And despite the continued difficulties of modern-day life, she always remained upbeat and optimistic.

Lucy Cross was her name and she became "Cenedl o Obaith - Nation of Hope."

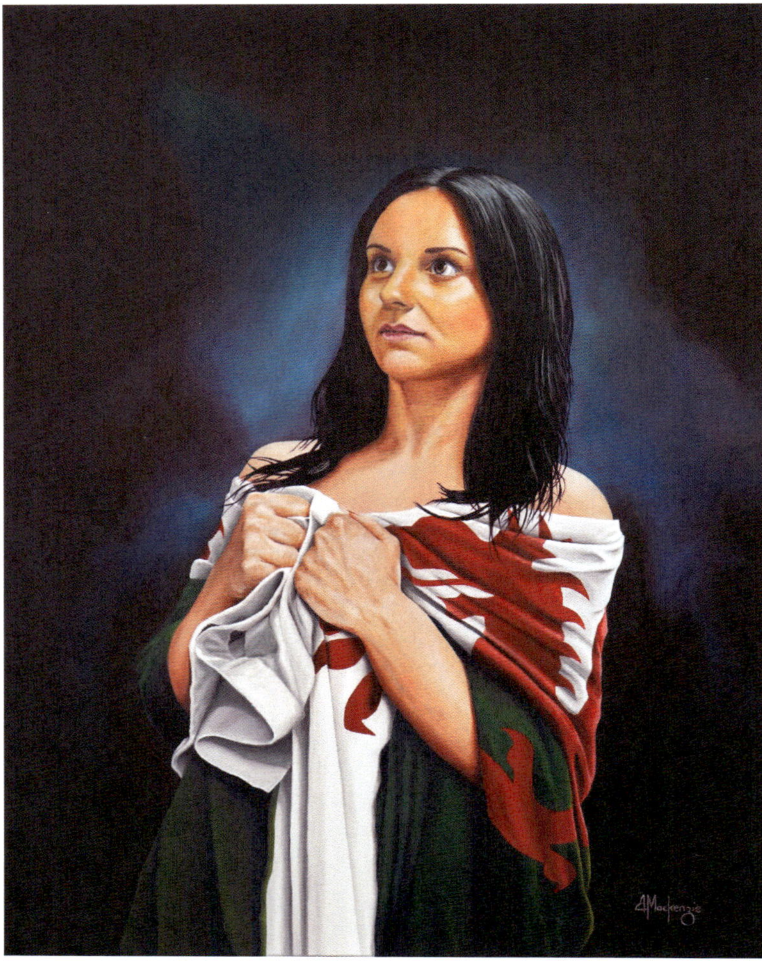

Cenedl o Obaith - Nation of Hope 71 x 91cm
by Ian Mackenzie

19

The Same Old Scene

As the years went by and I was exposed to life through the police, my experiences grew. Being constantly exposed to the depravity that society can drop to, started to come as little shock anymore. My initial astonishment of the way that people treated each other diminished. I became hardened to life's shameful side.

However, it did not detract from the main reason why I put myself in this position. By having to stand up to and deal with the absolute lowness that people stooped to, it truly challenged my own weaknesses of confidence and shyness. I had to continue creating a character for me to step into and overcome my problems.

I encountered many victims of terrible acts and recipients of despicable behaviour, from the simple thefts that deprived a sole family wage of food that week, to barbaric acts resulting in physical and psychological trauma, where death in some cases felt a simpler option for them than to face their new future as a victim.

I have many comical stories that I recount at parties and social events for family and friends, as well as exciting and thrilling encounters that keep my audience on the edge of their seats. However, it is probably the distressing incidents, the ones I avoid alluding to in jovial times, that I remember the most.

These were the real incidents that challenged my weaknesses and came to test my willpower, time and time again.

Sometimes, the fear was not born of a physical threat in front of me. On occasions the fear was that of something I perceived. If I told you I worked night shifts every week and that I was in fact afraid of the dark, I guess you would laugh. But there was never a truer word spoken. Oh, how I hid behind that settee as a kid when Dr Who was on TV, frightened out of my skin, but I had to watch.

Yes, I was the Police Officer who after an evening shift would ride his bicycle home at 2am as fast as he could along a darkened lane, past the local cemetery, purposefully not looking for the fear of becoming a victim of a Hammer House Horror film of the 1970s. Even now, I glance out of my kitchen window at night and try to stop myself worrying about what is hidden outside looking back at me

But over time, being exposed to the harder side of life is character building to say the least. It certainly was not the romantic goodies versus baddies image that many of us had when we joined the profession. With this, comes the skills to deal with far more than just the incident in front of you. In many cases, retired Police Officers are sought after commodities because of their astuteness, resilience and problem-solving abilities. They bring a different dimension to the table, because for years they have been at the beck and call of society to help people put their lives back together and negate the evil that cruelly targets the weak.

When society called, the police came, whether they wanted to or not. What is vastly different to most professions is the fact that there was no one else to solve that problem. The police could not choose whether to attend or not, or once there, decide that they did not want to be there and leave. They were and always will be the last bastion.

Perhaps this factor alone forced another change in me. The fact that these people had no one else to solve their problem, they called for me and I could not go anywhere until I sorted it, right then and there.

Of course, in a lot of cases we were loathed as we were the ones that made decisions on a discrepancy, a disagreement or an act of violence that were not always to everyone's preference. Naturally, we were going to upset someone's day.

In reflecting on how I had coped with the violence and cruel aspects of real life, I looked at all the incidents that I had dealt with, and how my organization had adapted and changed over time. The technology had certainly advanced and the modern police force was now unrecognizable from what it was years before. Older officers in service would comment that "it was never like that in my day." Certain sections of the public would state that they never see a Police Officer on the streets anymore. More and more, the paperwork to complete an incident or a case was increasing. However, so were the computer systems and communication networks. Working practices now existed between different agencies that once would have been shunned.

If crime decreased, then we were winning. We were locking up the bad guys and keeping the peace on the streets. The bosses would be happy, and the politicians could sing from the rooftops of their influence and their successful strategies, whilst the wheels of the criminal justice system kept turning.

But crime never really decreased. If one type of crime lowered through, for example, an improved manufacturing design, another area of crime would increase. Better designed cars reduced their theft, but stolen pedal cycles went through the roof. An improvement in computer software increased detection rates, whilst other software and platforms resulted in online hate crime. It appeared that it was Groundhog Day, and nothing really changed.

Within the Police Unit at the National Assembly, we had modified working practices and introduced armed police to the estate. Having spent a good proportion of my career in this role and environment, the change was not that different for me. For some, especially the more naïve members of the political establishment, this proved a shock and a worry. Suddenly, the threat that we faced felt real and current.

It had me thinking. I had a picture emerging in my artistic mind of a figure of authority looking out over a sea of pandemonium, trying to come to terms with what was happening.

One morning at the National Assembly, a uniformed colleague, Becks Williams came into work with her hair made up in a French braid. It looked so intricate, detailed and carefully woven, with each braid entwined immaculately. I knew that this was the image I was after, one to challenge the stereotypical male which dominated this specific role. Modern, well equipped, and ready to face the current threat and risks of our society today, she, like the painting "Cenedl o Obaith - Nation of Hope," would represent a contemporary civilization, upholding the law and diminishing evil.

The question of what she would be looking at was difficult and took time to develop. In fact, it was months before I could settle on a satisfactory image. I wanted it to reflect the many aspects that the police deal with throughout their careers.

The equipment and the procedures improved in that time. However, the behaviour did not. No matter what measures you put in place, no matter how many people you locked up and threw away the key, they just kept coming and filling those roles. It was the same with victims of domestic violence, public disorder, drug and gun crime and acts against the state, to name a few. The same criminal intent continued, with the same criminal mindset.

One aspect of modern policing is surveillance, and society is well versed in the CCTV world, which has now crept into the art of entertaining us all at times. This officer, I decided, would be viewing the world through CCTV, an operation of the modern Police Service.

If, through the length of a Police Officers career, criminal intent had not improved, and it was the same behaviour that they were watching, irrespective of the span of time, then regardless of what the officer is watching the behaviour through, it was the same old criminal activity. Old television sets stacked one on top of the other, as if left on a rubbish tip, represented this throw back.

Technology had moved on, systems had improved, but attitudes and behaviour had not. The image was clear. "The Same Old Scene" was created.

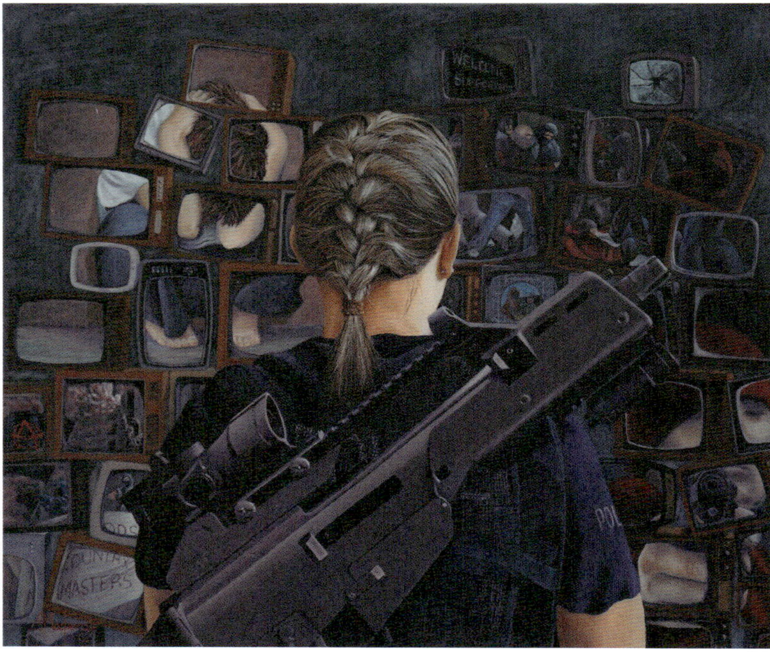

The Same Old Scene 69 x 60cm by Ian Mackenzie

20

Blind Justice

Within the National Assembly for Wales estate, our Police Unit worked with the utmost of confidence and therefore had restricted access to our office to very few trusted individuals. For both security and entertainment reasons, if you were not coming to see us with an interesting incident to report to us, or some good old-fashioned gossip, then access was not generally permitted. That basically summed up the criteria for entry.

In this environment we were able to discuss matters of utmost importance, openly and confidentially amongst ourselves. Issues of National Security and the safety of this political estate were vital. Equally important was the discussion and planning of my next art project.

With such in mind, following lunch one day, whilst quietly sat in my office, I heard an exacerbated voice commenting about the "bureaucracy of it all". It was coming from the main Police Unit office, muffled and distant, I was not fully sure who it was.

My seat was warm and comfortable and did nothing to help me wake from my light slumber. I just went with the flow, slipping further from the reality of work. The voice now expanded and contracted in pulsing waves of sound as if it were a radio station losing and gaining its frequency.

Suddenly, from the muffled sound, I recognised the accent and more to the point, the speaker. It was one of the Police Unit Officers, Geoff Moss. Even more to the point, he was stood at my office door pulling at police cordon tape that was wrapped around his head saying, "I can't do a thing boss. I'm stuck. Where's the justice, where's the justice?"

I immediately woke from my slumber with the sole aim of freeing Geoff from his worrying dilemma. I looked in his direction towards the door where he had stood, but I could not see him. He was not in the doorway. In fact, it was not the office doorway that I was staring at. Neither were the walls decorated as they should be with standard dull inoffensive non-political Assembly office grey paint.

Geoff was nowhere to be seen or heard. Neither were any other Police Officers or members of staff from the National Assembly for Wales come to think of it. Why would they be?

I was not in the office. I was nowhere near it. I was sat at home in my comfortable chair in front of the TV on a cold winter Saturday afternoon, a hot water bottle supporting my aching back, watching nothing in particular, following my usual predictable weekend lunch.

Somehow, without any conscious thought whatsoever, a random word from a partially heard TV programme had triggered a shard of inspiration deep inside my mind. It had activated my creativity, and a ripple effect had commenced. I had not even needed to consciously think to develop this image in my mind. It was there right in front of me, ready to be captured on canvas.

The difficult part was to act quickly enough to make sure the whole of the image was recorded, so that when the opportunity arose sometime in the future the figure would be clear and the reason I would be creating this artwork would not be lost.

Before I knew it, my head was full of images surrounding this word, and I was running with my next artistic idea. The word 'bureaucracy' had hit a chord somewhere deep in my subconscious and stimulated a previously dormant notion that was waiting for such a wakening. I reached for my pen and notebook and recorded my daydream.

I had my next art picture to create. I would require a few props to photograph and sketch and, of course, someone to sit and play the part. Who better than the actual person who my mind had thrown up post-lunch that random Saturday afternoon, causing me to reach for the notebook and record my vision?

Geoff Moss was a member of the Police Unit at the National Assembly for Wales, and a positive guy who volunteered for anything. The following week when I discussed my proposal, he happily offered to pose for photographs as to sit for a portrait by me would be the greatest endurance ordeal that anyone could face. I did not paint quickly.

Being responsible for the counter terrorist search regime part of the protection of the National Assembly estate, I knew every nook and cranny. So, one quiet Monday morning, Geoff and I headed off together with a third colleague, Rob Liles, to the Pierhead Building and the converted attic space which now lay vacant.

We rigged up a desk full of trays of overdue paperwork, important files of evidence and police equipment, similar to a desk in a divisional police station. We added a load of property items and personal issue kit as well. Soon, we had our 'crime scene.' Geoff dressed in his daily uniform, sat behind the desk, and started to look busy as I commenced taking photos.

It was not long before the creativity started to flourish. Amongst other items, I had a reel of police cordon tape which we used to wrap around the desk, depicting a crime scene incident. I looked at Geoff with the tape and thought back to my previous image. If this painting is about the bureaucratic nightmare hindering a good, hard-working Police Officer from doing his job, then he can't see the wood from the trees. What if he can't see because the police cordon tape is wrapped around his head and covers his eyes? A tool designed to assist in his role representing the bureaucracy itself. The very image I had dreamt of.

The image was clear. We rearranged Geoff and bound his head with the cordon tape, and I started photographing him again. He took to the role instantly and shook his head from side to side with the frustration that despite having all the equipment he needed to carry out his role, he was desk-bound by the need to support the departments that support him.

I asked him to take hold of the cordon tape at the side of his head and pull it in frustration, trying to break free. He pulled and pulled, and I took shot after shot. The tape stretched and stretched. He pulled more, I shot more, and the tape stretched more. We were all trying to remain sensible, but the situation was surreal and hilarious.

It summed up our careers in one moment. The willingness to try, the push to the limit, the bureaucracy, the apprehension, the tension. It was all there. And then the tape snapped.

The three of us burst out laughing at each other. A surreal moment when police, politics and art all came together. I altered the settings on the camera and played back the photographs. There, at the very end of one hundred shots was the one, the actual one that captured everything. The very last shot. It was the one that would form the basis of my artwork that could not be called anything other than 'Blind Justice.'

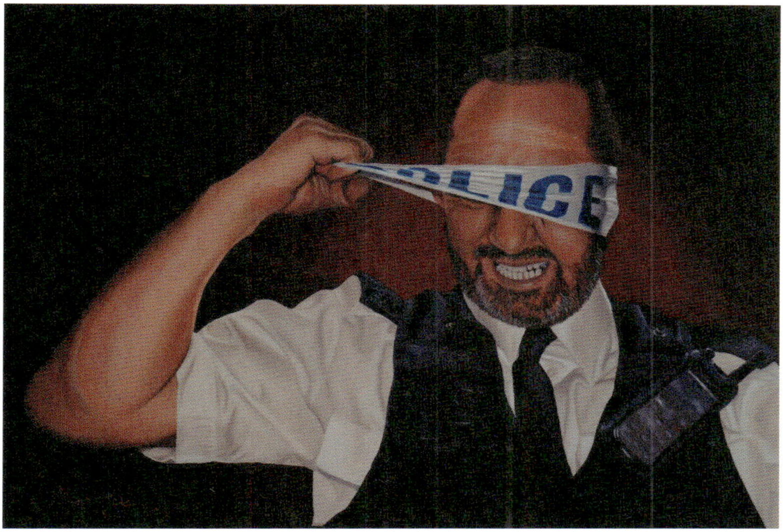

Blind Justice 59 x 42cm by Ian Mackenzie

21

The Chief

It was a career defining moment when I was asked to paint Peter Vaughan, the Chief Constable of South Wales Police. He was the highest-ranking Police Officer in the force, and my ultimate boss. This was probably the greatest artistic challenge that I had faced at that time, in more ways than I could have known.

At the National Assembly for Wales, people got to know me quite well as our role within this environment was unique. Having a Police Unit on hand in a public building full of politicians, journalists, lobbyists, and anarchists was always going to be a hazardous situation to keep an even keel.

As the Inspector, I was called upon continually to advise political leaders and their staff in the strictest of confidence, of ways to keep them safe whilst they pursued their agendas, at the same time as managing the expectations of opposition parties and the Assembly, who would have given anything to find out what their counterparts were planning.

The belief that the Police Unit led a risky and exciting day to day existence certainly raised our profile on the estate and helped to create an air of mysticism around us. With growing trust and respect, it was a refreshing change from being on the streets, where in the main we were treated like rubbish and abused every single day in one way, shape or form.

As such, I got to know quite a few people very quickly. In time, I was also known for my artwork, and I was asked to exhibit in the Assembly's restaurant. To a lesser few, I was known for my activity in the karate world. One person in particular who approached me with an interest in the latter, was the manager of the maintenance team, Kelvin Williams, who I was starting to get to know quite well.

In chatting with him, he soon became a member of my karate club based in Cardiff and would train regularly with us. I also came to know him as the close friend of the South Wales Police Chief Constable, Peter Vaughan.

The Chief was someone who was held in high regard by everyone he met. I met Peter, who was then a Custody Sergeant, when I was a member of the Priority Policing Team (a plain clothed street crime unit in Canton, Cardiff) back in the early 1990s. I recall his enthusiastic guidance as I and a colleague were lodging the most recent criminal miscreant we had caught, in the cell complex which he was managing. It was over-spilling with activity. Solicitors demanding access to individuals, officers struggling with detainees in every corner, parents waiting to give their offspring a clip round the ear or more in some cases, and us interrupting a career intent criminal, making his way in his chosen profession.

Peter would declare that he had no idea what he was doing as he opened a paper record to start the person's detention. This comment was a massive understatement, given the fact that he went on to successfully run our organisation in the top position for many years. We would relate the facts of the offence, whilst the accused would rant for his God-given right to a solicitor, a telephone call, the doctor, his dinner and anything else that society allowed him to have access to, without one single worry about the trail of devastation or victims that he had just created.

Peter would then send us back out to go and lock up more of these criminals, telling us to take them off the streets in order to protect the public, their cars and their homes.

Later, he became my Inspector for a short period when I was a Community Constable in Grangetown, Cardiff, when again he encouraged myself and colleagues with his go and get them attitude. No wonder he became the most popular Chief Constable of our force in modern times.

Now, as I became accustomed to the intricate balancing act of politics and police at the National Assembly, I would receive a call from the Chief's driver John Marshman, stating that he was bringing the Chief to meet with a political leader. John became a valuable cog in assisting me to keep the wheels in motion between the political heavyweights and the high-ranking Police Officers visiting this strange environment I was in.

I recall many instances, where characters from both organisations would attempt to jeopardise my plan, my day and my career with their antics, their personality clashes and their mischievous ways. Sometimes I think that they were all in collusion to see who could create the biggest spanner for me, the smallest player in their vastly important day. But those are stories for another time.

So, I would find myself quite often hosting the Chief in my office as he awaited the politicians. Of course, with my artwork in the restaurant as well as my room, he became inquisitive about my hobby. His mate Kelvin would call in and the banter would start. The failure of Kelvin in his next karate grading would obviously result in me being posted to the converted broom cupboard next to the Chief's office in Police Headquarters. That was always a good one to start with.

I would remind Kelvin that working from a broom cupboard next to the Chief's office may result in me devising some very difficult and punishing training sessions, and such a move would be detrimental to his physical wellbeing the next time we trained together. I was back in the ring.

I recall one early morning conversation with Kelvin, as we caught up over a cup of tea before the day kicked off in earnest. He asked if I would consider painting his mate's portrait. Yes, the Chief Constable's portrait. The immediate joke was that the painting was for him to put in his window to keep the burglars from paying him an unwanted visit. However, believe it or not, this was a genuine request and it had come from the Chief and his wife. I was honoured to have someone in such a high position to trust me with this responsibility. I was also quite nervous of such a request, as this could be the moment of balance between a successful career and one which drastically cascades downhill from this point onwards.

The film 'The Italian Job' came to mind, with the scene of the coach perched precariously on the edge of the cliff, as it rocks one way then the next, with the stolen gold at one end, and the characters at the other balancing their fate. That was me, indeed.

But there was no point in dithering and being indecisive anymore. I took the plunge and said I would do it. What could possibly go wrong? I needed to arrange to visit the Chief and take some photographs to work from, but I realised that I would have to book an appointment with him. I had no idea who he had told of this request, if anyone at all, besides his wife and Kelvin. I was conscious that this could go very wrong from the start, as not anyone could just ring up and book to see the Chief. My first dilemma.

Of course, I needed to check on my art 'Business Interest' renewal with the Professional Standards Department, which was a prerequisite to doing anything outside of the police world that may bring the organisation into disrepute. They had been dragging their heels this year. I had registered this business interest with the crazy idea that someday my art would take off and I would be inundated with work to carry out in my spare time. Maybe they too knew, as the Career Advisor did all those years before, that there was no future in art. Consequently, they were more interested in chasing other more significant issues rather than the form I had again submitted into the bureaucratic mechanism. My second dilemma.

Without raising a pencil or brush, I had a problem. Kelvin was away on holiday and I didn't want to delay this any longer than necessary. You just don't keep people this high up the ladder waiting.

So, I rang the Chief's Personal Assistant to book an appointment. Nerves kicked in and my palms began to sweat. It was only a phone call, I told myself, and get a grip. The Chief was asking me, not the other way round. His PA answered and immediately recognised me from previous conversations, when I had rung regarding his visits to the Assembly. So why should I be so nervous?

And then, the question came. "Why do you want an appointment Ian?"

"Because he asked me to ring and book an hour with him," I replied.

"And the reason?" Silence.

"Ian, the reason?"

"A personal reason."

"And the personal reason?"

I was not going to get away with it. I could not do it. I had to give the reason. Imagine lying and being found out that you had tried to book a meeting with the Chief for some totally made up excuse, albeit that you were trying to be confidential. What a comical conundrum. And so nervously, I confided in the Chief's PA. I recall her giggling at my dilemma, saying that it was fine, and she would book the appointment and looked forward to seeing me on the day.

She did ask me if I was bringing my paints. I cheekily replied that I would only need flesh tone, and I had now divulged too much to her about the type of portrait he had asked for.

Now to do battle with the Professional Standards Department without letting them know as well. I emailed repeatedly and it was only after them answering a personal call and me dropping the Chief's name that I made progress.

Subsequently, with a batch of photographs, a few conversations and several months of painting and contemplating how young I should make my newest model, I completed the task. The last of all the dilemmas, which is always worry regardless of who the artwork is for, is the hand over. Needless to say, that both the recipient and his wife were over the moon with the result. I had not put a year on his looks, and as such my role at the National Assembly was extended a little longer!

To chase a dream and get the role that I have worked very hard for, and then to be requested personally by the head of that organisation to paint their portrait, is an accolade that I am proud of.

The painting "The Chief" is definitely one of the most important portraits to date, for a number of reasons.

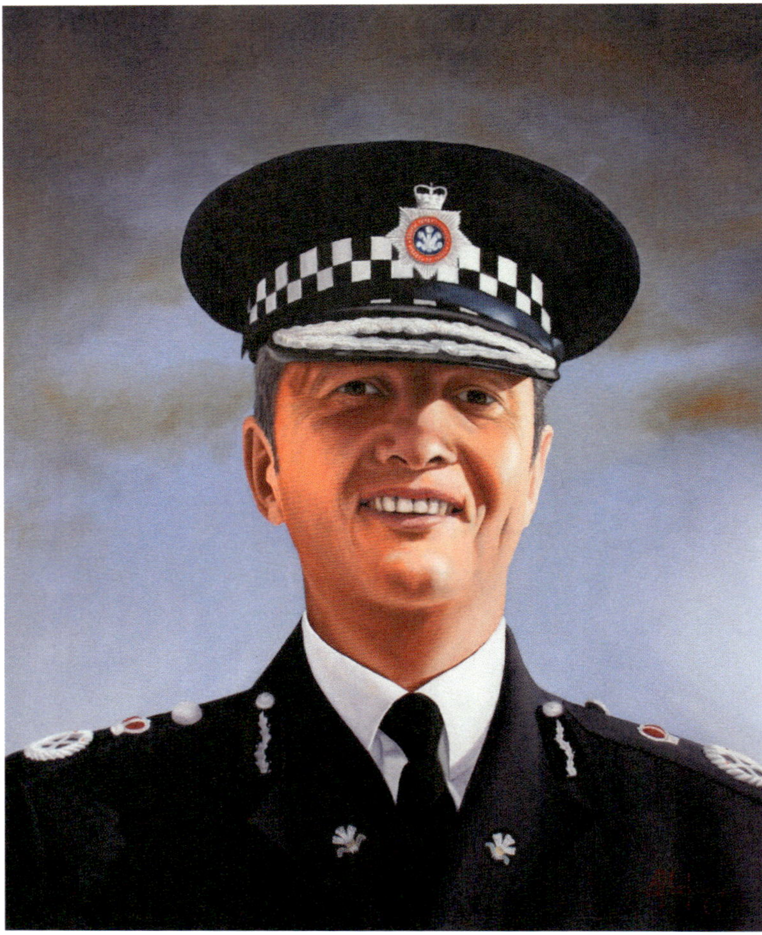

The Chief 41 x 51cm by Ian Mackenzie

22

Rod, Penny, and the Artist from Wales

Well there I was, one quiet Sunday afternoon, sat at the in-laws house with my wife enjoying some garbage TV, trying to stay awake, when through a slumbering misty haze I recognised a face on TV being interviewed, sat with a furry bundle of fluff on her lap.

I only took half took notice as my brain reluctantly received messages from my partially opening eyes. However, I became acutely aware of sharp dig in my left side as my name was called. I was sat in the same seat I had occupied for the last thirty years of visiting the in-laws. The message hit home, pay attention, it is the wife communicating with me in her usual way. It must be important.

"You could paint that," I heard. I looked at the TV. There on the screen was Penny Lancaster, wife of Rod Stewart, the greatest voice in rock'n'roll history. She was sat with a small ball of fur perched on her lap.

"Ian, I said you could paint that," came a second statement, obviously invoking a response which was still too quick for my brain to comprehend.

"Yes," I mumbled.

"No, you could paint that dog," came the reply.

"Yes, I know I could"

"Well why don't you?"

That was strange. The last time Tracy had concerned herself with what I painted was accompanied by the comment of why did I have to paint beautiful women and why couldn't I paint flowers or 'stuff like that'? Well stuff like that was not my stuff and I would leave that stuff to those who enjoy that stuff. I don't.

So, this was a rather strange experience I was starting to become wrapped up in. Well why don't I? Mmm. Why don't I just paint a dog that was on a TV programme on a Sunday afternoon at the in-laws? I was confused. Could I paint that dog? Could I paint any dog? Could I paint that dog there on the TV, sat on the lap of that woman?

I stared at the TV. Yes, it was all coming together. Penny Lancaster, the wife of the singer I had idolised as a young teenager, had a pet dog sat on her lap. I had built up a considerable reputation for applying my artistic skills in painting pets ever since members of the South Wales Police Dog Section attended at the National Assembly for Wales and saw my artwork on the wall. There had been an endless stream of requests for their canine family members to be captured forever in oil paint on canvas and hung in their homes with pride. I was enabling owners to extend their emotional bond and help create memories and stories to live well into the future.

There were a large number of people who love their pets, more than their own family members in some cases. I had taught myself a way of creating portraits through trial and error to a standard that I was confident enough for people to enjoy. It was always a test of nerves painting for someone else. However, over time I learned that with each painting there is a continual improvement in the managing of planning, drawing, colour, shape, varnishing and a host of other aspects that go into the lengthy process of photorealism art.

So, I could do it. I could actually paint to a sufficient standard that I would be happy to present to someone such as Rod Stewart and Penny Lancaster as it would be the best that I could do, and they could receive.

However, my issue was how on earth would I get a painting like that to them? In the back of my mind, I had a memory of a conversation that had taken place not too long ago. I had been in Harlow on a weekend karate course, where I had been teaching for two days. I was known throughout our organisation for what I would refer to as my musical taste and of course my spikey hair. So, it came as no surprise that during the evening, the conversation of Rod Stewart came up. I was chatting with a friend and local instructor by the name of Robbie Hutchin.

He asked if I knew that Rod had recently moved to a new house, to which I replied that I had heard something. Well, he stated, the house that he had moved to was directly at the back of his carpentry business. We both laughed as I commented how fortuitous that was, and that one day I may come calling for a favour. He comically told me that he wanted nothing to do with any stalking offences, to which I said I would get him anonymity and police protection. We both laughed.

I trawled the internet looking for a connection with Rod's agency and found links to California and the likes. I thought that if I was to create this artwork, which would take me the usual thirty hours of work over three months, this was a lot of effort for it to be sent to the United States, with no real hope of it being passed back to England, let alone get to their home address. However, that conversation with Robbie rung in my mind. It was worth revisiting.

Now, there is a lesson here. If you ever come across someone who is helpful and willing to go that extra mile to assist you, never forget them. These individuals far outweigh all the negative people that try to keep us down and in lowly places.

I contacted Robbie and asked if I could request a favour of him. He immediately said yes and subsequently, a plot was hatched. I had already started the painting, as I was determined to get this to Rod and Penny somehow, regardless. Now I had my contact, who not only within moments of messaging him passed their address to me, but also said that he would take the item there and deliver it in person to their home. I could not ask for more.

The painting was finished, varnished, packed, and sent to Robbie, with the offer of creating a portrait of his own pet dog for his very generous action. I waited to hear of his endeavour.

A few days later, I had a text to tell me that Rod had a noticeably large gate. I laughed out loud and replied, "Do your best."

A response came back. Brazenly, Robbie had done it. He had got beyond the large gate and had spoken to a person who appeared as the Head of Security for the estate. He had explained my story and was assured that the artwork would be well received. Mission accomplished. I was excited to say the least. However, this story did not end there.

Five days later, my family and I were sat about ten rows from the front of the latest Rod Stewart open air concert in Milton Keynes. Eagerly anticipating yet another show, we watched the support acts as the stadium filled. Having attended over thirty of his concerts since my teenage years, on numerous occasions I had been fortunate enough to purchase tickets at the very front of the shows, either through the fan club or by sheer belligerence on the internet booking systems. However, this was close and a great view.

Connor and I were making our way back to our seats having visited the bar before the main show started. We noticed an entourage had arrived and filled the vacant area in front of us. We looked a second time and saw exactly who this was. Penny Lancaster, her two sons and a group of family and friends. My immediate thought was Rod Stewart, you cheapskate. Those seats are not even the most expensive. The front three rows are, and you have not put your own family in them.

However, it dawned on me. I was a short distance away from them and Connor, the eternal optimist, whispered in my ear "You've got to do it." I knew that this was the one and probably only moment that I would ever come close to an opportunity like this. Everything was pointing in the one direction. I had spent months painting their dog Bubbles, I had found a contact to assist me, and if Robbie had gone out of his way to help me with this crazy idea, had the nerve to get into the Stewart estate and walk up to the front door, then the least I could do was to try and put one foot forward and say hello.

Time stood still and my brain went into overdrive. I never thought that I would be in this position, but now I was going to have to put all my policing skills into action and breach the security around this group.

"I'm going," I told Connor and I stepped forward. In my mind the eyes of the entire stadium were on me I thought. I ignored one security guard after another as I weaved through the entourage, getting closer and closer. Suddenly, I was stood in front of the main security personnel for Penny. I was aware that she was directly behind him. He turned, raised his hand, and said, "No photographs."

I then went into my unrehearsed spiel. I said that I did not want to take a photograph, but I had had a painting I created delivered to their home address only five days ago. I named their home. The painting was of their dog. I named their dog. I wanted to make sure that Penny was happy with the standard of the artwork. Where on earth that came from, I had no idea. He looked perplexed, and with a wry smile, turned to Penny.

With that, I saw her lean around his body from her seated position and immediately start talking to me. In a moment she was telling me that they loved the painting of Bubbles and was introducing me to her mother. I could not believe it. There I was in the middle of the Stewart family discussing my artwork whilst we waited for the main show to start. Furthermore, Penny's mother momentarily threw me. She introduced herself as Rods mother-in-law, but in fact looked younger than Rod himself.

In this surreal moment, time continued to stand still. Penny's mother told me that they had read the letter I had enclosed with the artwork and referred to them both discussing the time and layers involved in creating the painting of their dog. What was I doing? What was going on? This does not happen to people like me.

But alas, no sooner had the encounter started than it ended, as the show commenced, and Rod burst out onto the stage in front of us. I gave my thanks to them and returned to my family a few rows behind. I know that Rod opened the show with the song "Infatuation," but don't ask me what else he sang that night, what he wore or anything else of our stay in Milton Keynes, I do not have a clue.

What I do have is a memory of a dreamlike situation that had started with a suggestion, an application of a talent and the coming together of positive people to make something happen.

Some people are said to be lucky and always fall on their feet. However, if you do not create the situations in the first instance for such luck to find you, then sorry, it will not happen.

This is the prime example of making your own luck. "Bubbles" was that luck.

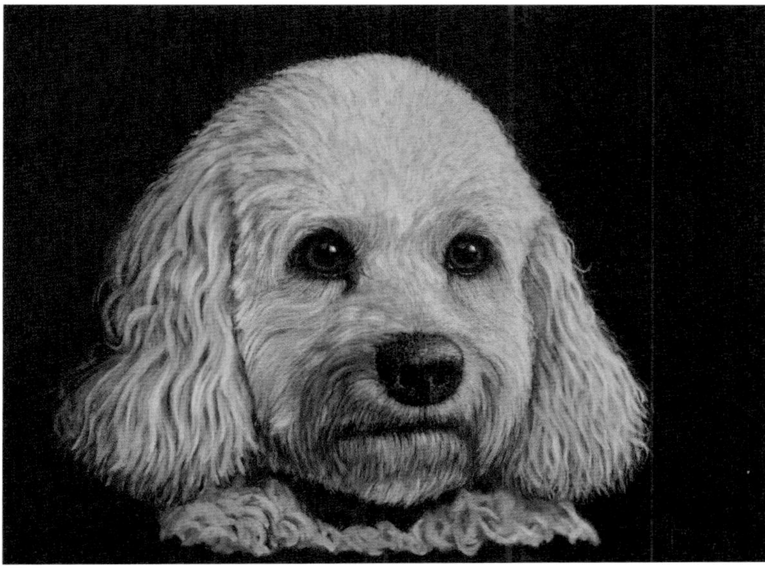

Bubbles 41 x 30cm by Ian Mackenzie

23

Gareth Bale is "Y Ddraig Rhuodd - The Dragon Roared"

One of the possible ways to make it in this world of art would be to enter a competition, win the competition and be heralded as the new Salvador Dali or Mitch Griffiths of oil painting. It was that simple. I just needed the right competition, with the right judges and the right prize, and my art career would take off.

So, when I noticed that the Cric Gallery in Crickhowell, Powys, was hosting their next competition and it was open to all artists, I decided that this was the one. I was even more convinced when I saw they had a special category named Welsh Legends. I knew the very subject who personified the word legend like no other. One person who currently featured in the media and in the minds of the whole nation. This was so much my competition, it was not fair on anyone else, they might as well just award me the prize now and be done with it.

This national icon was the captain of the most successful Welsh football team of our time. The semi-finalists of the recent Euro 2016 competition, full of individual heroes joined together in the common cause and led by the inspirational Real

Madrid icon and first one-hundred-million Euro transfer fee player, Gareth Bale. The legend from the local Whitchurch High School in Cardiff who had made it to the big time. Yes, Gareth Bale was going to be my entry for the Welsh Legends competition and win me my rightful place in this world of modern art.

Around this time there were comments in the press regarding the Welsh flag and it was being strongly proclaimed as the world's finest design. Of course, three million unbiased judges would not disagree with any individual who came to that conclusion. As such, it would be only fitting to incorporate a flag featuring a mighty fictional beast within my artwork. It could only enhance the sensational impact that this footballer, as one of the top three iconic players in the world at that time, had on a team, an international football contest and of course the art competition that I was going to win.

My image was starting to emerge in my mind and took several preliminary sketches to measure correct lengths of limbs, body parts and the amalgamation of two images into one winning entry. This idea was going to be so iconic, so current that upon opening my entry, the judges might as well take the rest of the day off.

Of course, there would be the national press to handle and the subsequent selling of the winning piece as well. Perhaps I should consider a limited edition set of giclee prints. I just wondered if I would be available when Gareth rang to congratulate me and ask for his own original piece commissioned for his Spanish mansion. I would have to deliver it to him in person obviously, that is only good manners and what he would naturally expect from one icon to another, especially if he wished the artwork to be flown out as soon as it was ready…

Oh, how the imagination runs wild, firstly in creating potentially iconic art if ever I could, and then getting totally side tracked in pure fantasy, and the two end up becoming a mixture of what is possible and probable and what is downright make-believe. But it could possibly happen to someone somewhere, and if that were the case, why not me?

After all, I am the one who started the thought process, I am the one who can create the artwork, so why would it not be me? If you believe in it, it will happen. I live by this and I will die by this and one day my belief will be reality.

I was once privy to a senior Welsh Government Minister telling a group of members of the press about a decision she had made and the process which she had used to come to that decision. She stated that she was right, she had always been right, and she would continue to be right until everyone agreed that she was right in the first place. There is nothing like self-belief. In the right hands of course.

So, the work was coming on nicely and on time. I needed to look at the competition application process, not that I needed to enter as the gallery would probably hear of my renown and come direct to me, hailing my success well before the date of submission.

However, I had better apply just in case. I waited for the piece to be finished and then I commenced the onerous process of submitting information. Each gallery has its own requirements, and this was just as unique. A good quality photograph makes all the difference and ensures safe passage to the final exhibition stage as well as correctly written application details, CV and biography and Artists Statement. Anything else I hear you ask?

Cutting, cropping, shrinking, you name it, I was doing it. Gone were the days of me sitting in that classroom all on my own, happy as Larry, drawing my cowboy, getting excited as I added silver spurs and a wide brimmed hat, not a care in the world. I could not be further from that experience, frustration boiling over as I continually failed to correctly shrink the image to an acceptable size, internet connection waning, patience thinning and deadline moment approaching.

Finally, at the eleventh hour, it went. It was on its way. I was excited. This was the one, the painting of all paintings that I had created, albeit that I have and will continually say this with every piece of artwork I do. But this was the one.

No sooner had I submitted it than the announcement day was upon me. The phone was on loud, turned up for the call. The internet clear and active. And I sat and waited. Each hour I checked the various electronic communication devices which now dictate every move we make. And I sat and waited. In fact, I sat and waited and checked and sat and waited and checked all day long.

It was well into the evening when it dawned on me to look in my email junk folder. Yes, of course, my acceptance email will be there. I opened it, I looked through the listed rubbish. There it sat, halfway down the page. I clicked on it and it opened. I only had to read one word. It was the word that jumped out at me from the page. The word 'Unfortunately.'

I did not need to read any more. I could not believe it. This must be the wrong correspondence. I quickly checked the email list again, but no. This was the one and I had been rejected, no matter how many times I read the email in disbelief. Didn't they know that I had painted this masterpiece just for their show? That is how important this painting was. Researched, designed, sketched and painted all for one moment, for them and for no one else. What a failure I thought. The single most iconic person of the decade to hold the title of Welsh Legend, there is no one else.

How wrong I was. It taught me a great lesson, which was never to look at the title of an art competition and then create a piece of work to match what you think is intended by it. Art is very subjective and the interpretation of a title, phrase or even a single word can vary to the extreme.

But my story of this painting does not end there. It did not end up in the cupboard of rejection alongside other failed attempts at success. Following this moment, I had taken the decision to have a collection of prints made and mounted in case I was fortunate enough to have someone who was interested in this artwork as it hit my social media accounts. Sure enough, on an evening the Welsh football squad were playing at home, having posted some pictures, I had a message to contact an old friend of mine.

Mark Samuel was a colleague from my days as a Firearms Officer on the Area Response Group in South Wales Police. He had retired from his Sergeant's role and was now a civilian Firearms Instructor running courses and, in particular, management training at a well-known hotel and sports complex not far from my home.

He let me know of a possible scenario that could take place if I was up for it. I was gobsmacked. Of course, I would be willing, and we set up a meeting. Forty-eight hours later, having met Mark a little earlier, I was again sat at home by my mobile, my iPad and my computer, waiting, trying to put the possibilities of what may happen to the back of my mind. Positive things never really happened to the likes of me, I was not that fortunate. A cold winter's evening was about to get warm.

The phone pinged and there, brightly lit up for everyone to see, was a picture that Mark had just sent me coupled with the comment, "Mackenzie you owe me." The Welsh iconic legend Gareth Bale, was leaning over two mounted prints of the painting that I had created of him, signing not only them, but also the original artwork itself. He was taking care to delicately sign his name and his shirt number in the bottom corner.

Wow. I could not believe it. From the despair of being rejected from a competition to having the first million Euro football star actually sign a painting that I had created of him was unbelievable. And even more so, he gladly accepted the print that Mark handed to him of the painting of himself signed by me, with my thanks!

It just goes to show that rejection is not a failure. It is a re-assessment and redirection of your path in your story that you are shaping and moulding with positive people around you, supporting and guiding you all the way.

If you never give up trying, you never fail. The story of "Y Ddraig Rhuodd -The Dragon Roared" was complete.

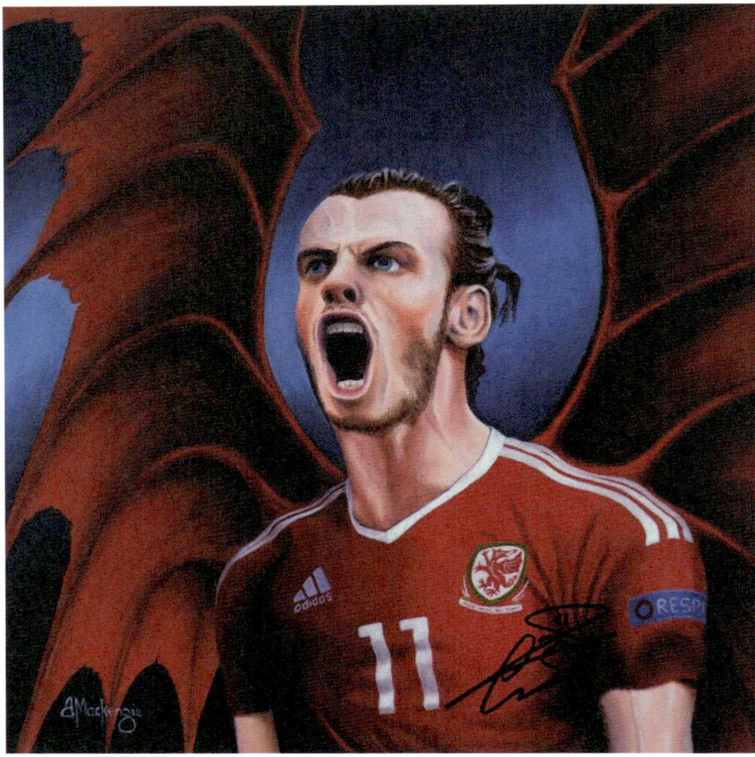

Y Ddraig Rhuodd - The Dragon Roared 41 x 41cm
by Ian Mackenzie

24

Photorealism and the Pussycat

So, in pushing yourself to the limit in whatever discipline you choose, there comes a time when the hard work pays off, and you achieve something that is pretty much close to perfection, if not perfection itself. It may be an activity that is rewarded in money, wealth, or even a gold medal at the highest level of physical activity, for instance. This moment may come in the form of attaining a successful position, or fame and lasting recognition, or of personal satisfaction that you and you alone cherish. For some, it could even be the creation of an item or a moment in time that makes people look with disbelief.

That moment when an object stops them in their tracks, and they cannot believe what is before them, their eyes wide open in wonder and awe. They cannot fathom what is before them and they question what they are looking at. Is it actually what they think it is?

In terms of photorealism art, that is the point when you have got them. Your artwork has made them stop, stare, and question what they see. Is that picture a photograph or is it a painting? Or even better, they assume it is a photograph until someone points out that it is not. Then it is the look of disbelief that wins the day.

The ultimate challenge for a photorealistic artist is to capture an image and create it in such a way that it is as close to the original item, that it looks exactly like the actual item or photograph. There are no errors, no brush strokes, and no abstract connotations. The person, the animal, the object, or the view is perfect, and the art of illusion is complete.

Now, studying how to do this is difficult and takes forever. It is not straight forward and the only way to get there is to keep painting and keep trying. I have never had a lesson on how to paint this way. I have never been told how to do it and have had to work out these methods by trial and error.

No matter what happens, I always start a painting with the aim to achieve this level each time. If, in some part of the artwork I get there, fantastic. I learn from it and apply the technique that I have just tried to the next painting I do of a similar subject. There are so many different types of materials on the market that you can use, it all comes down to preference.

However, the most important part in this process is how committed you are to achieving this goal. It is time consuming and very demanding on detail and perfection. Nevertheless, if perfection is your goal, then time is of no consequence. Perfection is.

So, I decided to aim high, having created several pieces of artwork that were getting closer to a photorealistic result. I threw all my skills at my next piece and was not going to stop until I had perfected it. If I never try, I will never know. I could potter around the outskirts of photorealism, opting out when a painting did not go as planned, and accept the result for what it was. I could settle for creating some abstract work that does not have to physically look anything like the object, the person, or the view. However, no. Now was the time to do it. To give it my best shot and spend the time and skills trying to create a photorealistic painting that I could be proud of.

With this realization, I had the opportunity to paint a showgirl by the name of Misha Hanlon, who my son Connor knew from his career as a musician. I had come to understand from visiting galleries in London that the larger the painting and the further you were away from it, the more photorealistic the result. But I did not want to start painting large canvases right now and be burdened with them and their imposing size, cluttering up the studio. The self-doubt and lack of confidence again coming to the fore and shaping my creativity once more.

I settled for a reasonable sized box canvas and started to sketch the basic facial shape. I started to paint thin layers taking my time, dipping in and out of it making sure that the layers of oil were drying each week. The detail was crucial and took its toll on my eyesight as I strained to make sure the mask Misha was wearing enhanced her face, and appeared to sit off the skin in places, with a shadow resting in the gap between.

After three months of painstaking work, repainting, and many thin layers of oil, it was ready. Following a drying period and varnishing, boy was I pleased. In terms of photorealism, this was by far the best painting I had created to date.

As people started to get a glimpse of it, my mission was complete. They found it difficult to see that it was in fact a painting. They queried themselves and their friends, arguing with one another, as I watched trying my best to hide my satisfaction. In one case, I had to produce the series of photographs I had taken, evidencing the painting process stage by stage. Job done, success. Now to keep this standard and push even higher.

I had raised the bar and I was challenging myself. I was focusing on something special, channeling the early negativity in my life in a positive direction. I could feel the excitement and see the change.

Where it was going to lead to, or how I was going to get there, I did not know. That did not matter. A specific line from a Rod Stewart song called 'Farewell' played over and over in my mind, and reminded me of this moment, *'Aim high, reach for the sky, how you gonna know unless you try.'*

What I did know was that my painting "Pussycat" was the springboard to aim high, and I had just jumped.

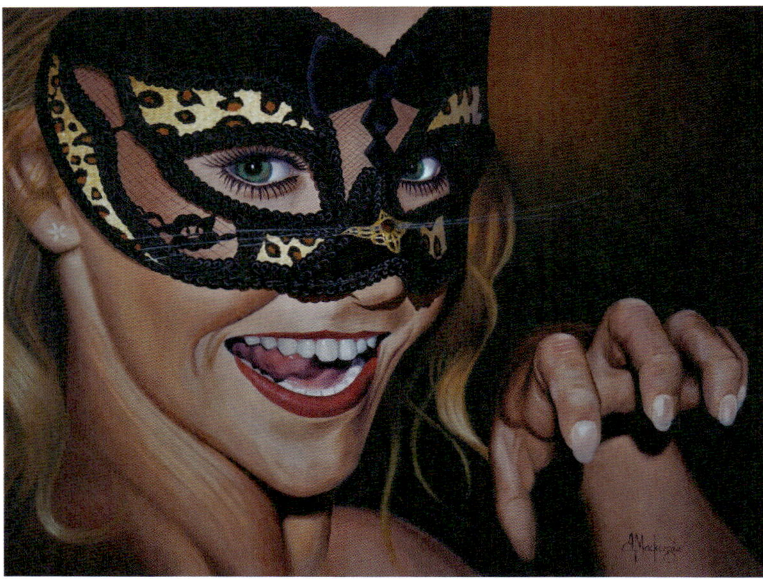

Pussycat 45 x 36cm by Ian Mackenzie

25

Think Like, Be Like

During my police career, I have been very fortunate to have experienced many different departments. From the early days of being in uniform on the streets of Canton and Grangetown in Cardiff, responding to calls from the public, to the latter years, dealing with the intricate requests of high flying and well connected politicians, there has been one skill that I have come to appreciate. This skill in fact was reiterated to me by the Presiding Officer himself, on my return to the National Assembly for Wales as the Police Inspector.

We would meet regularly and share the political news, the current police intelligence and terrorist threats, and of course the gossip. Lord Dafydd Elis-Thomas would often part with words of wisdom and guidance. He was a person of extreme influence and was well connected throughout the country. He had a wealth of knowledge that he could pull on at any time. In moments of trust and in confidence, he would also allude to his own fascinating political career, which is a story in itself.

In one of our regular one to one meetings, with passion and the whole weight of his political experience behind him, he said to me, "See, Inspector, I have learned over time, that in order to beat them, you have to become them, and beat them from within".

It reflected back to my early days when I would be known for catching thieves right in the act, whether they were breaking into cars, shops or acting suspicious. I earned a move to the plain clothed unit within my first station after two years' service by applying a simple principle. To catch a criminal, you must think like a criminal. You had to firstly observe and recognize that a person was up to no good. Then you had to put yourself in their position. What was your intention, what are you going to steal, how are you going to do it and where would you escape to?

The more I understood this concept, the easier it became to catch a certain type of individual. It was, for all intents and purposes, becoming a criminal to catch a criminal.

I recall one simple incident during an evening shift whilst on the plain clothed unit. A call came out about a burglary of a shop in progress. I drove one of our undercover cars to the vicinity where I believed these perpetrators would run to. Within a moment of arriving, driving through the lanes away from the scene, I recognized one of the burglars fleeing towards me. I waved to him and opened the passenger door. He got in and shouted "Drive, quick!" which I did. All the way to the Police Station.

Now, take the notion of thinking like a criminal to the extreme. Think of the most devastating aspects we face and apply the same principle. In my mind, this is the loss of life, by the action or inaction of another. Think of a person in a position of responsibility with the capability and power to be able to cause the loss of a life, or for that fact, to protect such a life. Then consider if you were in that position of protecting that life or taking it, what would your thought process be?

Within my police career, I was part of a firearms team and was armed for a number of years, dealing with criminals who at times were highly intent on carrying out their activities, high on drugs, possessed firearms and other lethal weapons. Thankfully, I have never had to discharge a firearm to protect or take a life. However, the question often arose. In order to protect the innocent, how far does your thought process take you to preempt the act that you face? How far do you become the villain in your mind to negate their action?

To explain this idea on a canvas, I took the notion of an armed Police Officer who is faced with a threat that is so extreme, he has to become the threat itself in order to negate it. In doing so, he walks that fine line between good and evil in this pursuit. He has all the equipment and training to allow him to make a valued judgement. The policies and incidents have placed him in that position. But he also has the psychological issues of making that decision which has repercussions that experienced officers with those skills know too well.

In doing so, he wears both the uniform of justice and virtue, as well as the vendetta mask of the anti-establishment groups, the anarchists and those that seek to bring terror to the innocent. The morphing of the two and the thin line this officer walks is a precarious psychological challenge for anyone in that position, and not for the faint-hearted.

A colleague by the name of Gareth Price from the Assembly Police Unit, who I must say stands firmly on the side of justice, donned the mask, and portrayed the concept of the thin line between good and evil.

"Think Like, Be Like" became an uneasy, but exciting challenge to capture.

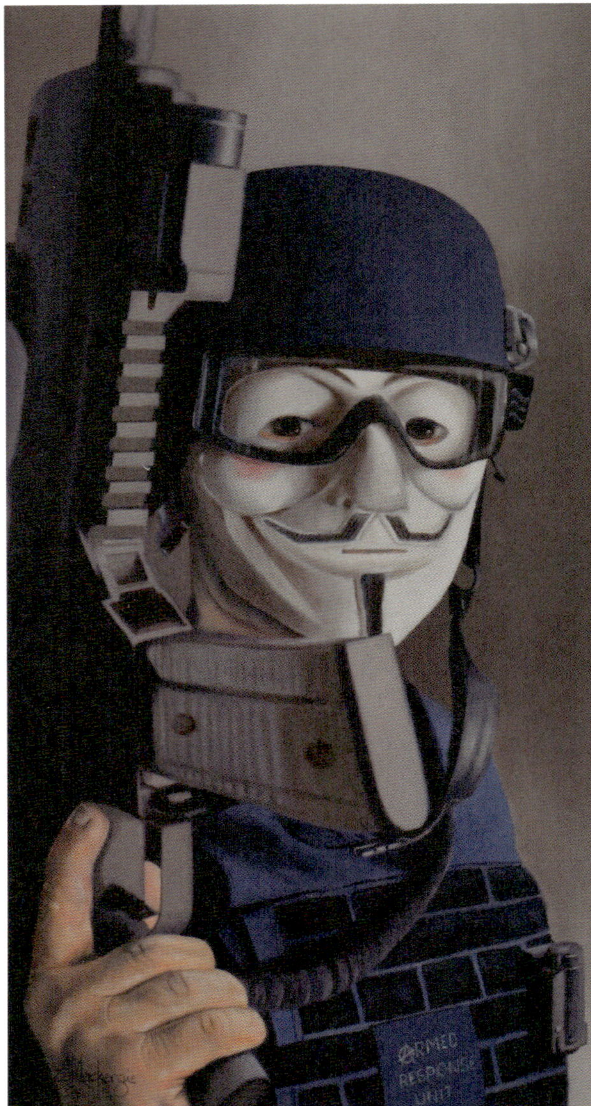

Think Like, Be Like 25 x 50cm by Ian Mackenzie

26

Once Upon a Time in the West

Quite a few people who have seen either of the paintings I have created called 'Once Upon a Time in the West I & II' have commented that they are very Dali-esque. This is a reference to Salvador Dali and the fantastic artwork he created in 1931 called 'The Persistence of Memory.' It depicts three melting pocket watches in a landscape scene, one of which hangs over a tree branch with a series of cliffs in the background.

In the autobiography *The Secret Life of Salvador Dali,* he explains that his inspiration for this work came from a dinner that included camembert. He became unwell with a migraine later that evening, which subsequently afforded him the idea of playing with the concept of "supersoft," changing a painting to include pocket watches, representing overripe melting cheese. This is probably his most famous work.

During a family holiday to Florida, I had the opportunity to visit the Salvador Dali Museum and see at first-hand his extraordinary artwork. The colours and the precision are fantastic, and the ideas behind his artwork are mind-blowing.

In terms of my own creativity, I can say that I enjoy painting with vibrant colours. I also I try to paint objects as accurately as I can. I too paint pocket watches, a subject just like this ingenious creator, and I have also suffered from debilitating migraines at times. However, for my particular artwork and the honour of being mentioned in the same breath as Dali, that is where this reference ends completely.

The real reason I painted the first of these two pieces of art is much simpler. Remember, I am not as clever and as deep in my thought process as you may think, and certainly would never in a million years come up with something as breath-taking.

I am the owner of several pocket watches and am always waiting for an opportunity to dress up and wear them. Coupled with the fact that as a child, I always liked a good western film, it was only appropriate that I should combine the two and create a scene that hints towards a story similar to those great cowboy films of the 1960s. 'For a Few Dollars More,' directed by Sergio Leone in 1965, the year of my birth, gave me the inspiration and the desire to test my skills of accuracy and storytelling.

The first painting was created with a cowboy on horseback appearing to leave the scene of a gunfight somewhere in the wild west. I painted it and proudly had it exhibited. I thought my work was done.

However, when I had the occasion to display this artwork at the National Assembly for Wales, home of Welsh politics, my good friend, Political Correspondent and familiar face of ITV, Gareth Hughes, cast his astute eye over it. As we sat at breakfast one morning, discussing the important issues pertaining to politics (i.e. gossip, innuendo and art) he made an observation.

"Lose the cowboy. It tells too much," he stated. I believe that a similar comment was once made in 'The Social Network' film by Sean Parker to Mark Zuckerberg. He said to lose the 'The' in 'The Facebook'!

So, I did. I set up the scene with my camera, my pocket watch, and my other hand. As with the first painting, I laid my hand out on the desk in front of me and placed the pocket watch in various positions in my grip. At the same time, I peered through my camera lens for the best photographic angle.

I must say that I am quite flexible and able to move limbs independently of each other. However, if you have ever set up a table-top scene and have your left hand as the starring role whilst your right is holding a camera to your face, attempting to negate the issues that come with closeness to a subject and camera shake, you will know exactly where this is going.

To make matters worse, I had to reverse the scene as I needed to create a picture that was the opposite to the first painting. This second one would just look the same and would not be worth doing if that was the case. Furthermore, my camera remained a right-handed click button mechanism. To ensure that I had the correct image, I would need to swap both hands and take these photographs remotely. Back to the drawing board to learn a new skill.

Finally, I had a series of images, all taken at eye level to give the viewer the sense that they were observing this as the victim of this incident, and this was their hand and time piece. What had happened to them would be down to their imagination. The artwork was created over the next few months and it hung proudly alongside 'Once Upon a Time I' in my studio. Would there be a third, I thought?

Perhaps with a little good fortune, having already created the first and taken good advice on story telling from Gareth, this new piece would tell less and intrigue more. I was learning bit by bit. Enter it into the right competition and I'll be away.

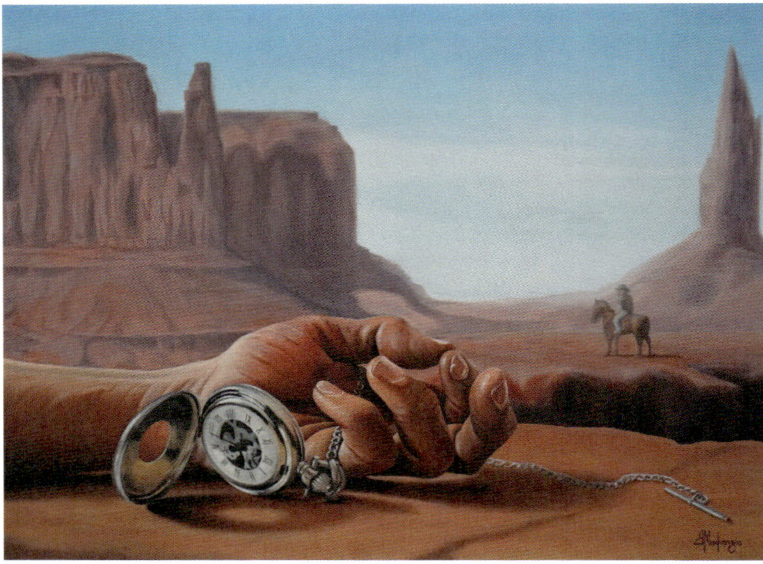

Once Upon a Time in the West I 51 x 46cm
by Ian Mackenzie

27

The Award Winning Artist

The new year had started, and my aim was clear. Time to again throw myself at my recently rekindled aim in life and make it as an artist. Just days before, I had met with Paul Wakefield, an inspirational entrepreneur, whose advice I had recently sought for my plight. Little did I know that fortune favours the brave and taking up Pauls offer for a one-to-one meeting was, upon reflection, the smartest business move I have ever made and the start of an incredible week.

Sunday morning and I was up early to continue the struggle with technology. I was battling with my computer and my iPad, which continually told me it was full and unable to function correctly. I simply wanted my music to play whilst I lost myself in creating my next masterpiece in the studio. Afterall, there was room in my cupboard for another failed canvas and I was going to fill it. There would also be room where my computer sat if it did not behave. My frustration was boiling over. What would probably appear simple to a computer whizz kid was dragging me down.

Earlier in the week, I had replied to an email sent by Jan Pennell, the owner of Y Galeri Caerphilly with her husband Gareth, confirming my attendance at their final exhibition day. I had entered their annual art show and was fortunately successful to be chosen to exhibit a painting as part of their annual event.

However, today was not going to plan. This computer problem was not going away no matter how much effort I put into staring and cursing at it. It was now eating into my art time and my creativity was not having any effect on it whatsoever. There is only a certain amount of magic that comes with the paintbrush, and the little black computer box under the study desk was not a willing participant.

Looking at my watch, I surrendered and went for lunch. Hurriedly, I reminded Tracy that we needed to get to the exhibition to support the fortunate winners of the current competition. As I reflected on the competitions that I had entered before, I had pretty much given up hope of winning anything in art these days. I had previously been placed sixth in a worldwide online competition for my painting called "Pussycat." I had also received other similar placings in online competitions, all of which went towards building my confidence and CV.

However, the endeavour of going through an online process and then delivering your successful artwork to a gallery, thereby overcoming the first hurdle, was different. The human element was exciting when you are part of a final show and invited to be present when the winner is revealed.

I had got to this stage many a time, always to be reminded of my place in this world, and to go back to continuing to strive and achieve better next time around. It was wearing to say the least, and it did cross my mind that this was going to be just another one of those events. I had second thoughts on attending. But such is life and there are others who need support, friends to meet and make, and who knows, the inspiration of other's art would no doubt drive me onwards. So, off we went.

We arrived to a gallery crammed full of people. Standing outside Y Galeri in Caerphilly town centre with my wife, looking through the glass door, I realised we were only just in time. A speech of some kind or announcement was taking place. I cautiously opened the door, trying not to disturb the proceedings. There was nowhere to go as people of all shapes and sizes in their winter overcoats filled the gallery to capacity. I turned and beckoned my wife to join me, but she declined. There was hardly any room for me to stand in the open doorway let alone anyone else.

I squeezed the door shut as a few people in front of me shuffled slightly. Having obviously experienced their own lateness and uncomfortable entry, they tried their best to make some room for me. Tracy moved to an outside window and peered in. The award ceremony had started. The gallery was so packed, I could hardly raise my hands to clap the announcements. I wished I had undone my coat. There was no chance now as the heat of the gathering rose.

Some artists were awarded Special Merit Certificates for their well-deserved efforts. I nodded approvingly looking around the immediate area at the few paintings I could see above everyone's heads. They were good. In fact, they were exceptional. Again, attending these events was both belittling and exhilarating. My lack of confidence came to the fore as I perceived my position amongst these fantastic artists. I would need to up my standard once more I thought. However, the excitement of seeing current artwork was inspiring and a reminder that perhaps I was not too far behind others. The distance, an incalculable one nonetheless, did concern and baffle me at the same time.

I continued trying to listen to the speech being made by the owner and the Town Mayor, just catching the occasional word and sentence. An award with a strange name was being introduced along with an explanation of why a specific artwork had been chosen. Someone will be pleased with it I thought.

"And for 'One Upon a Time in the West II,' the winner is …… Ian Mackenzie."

I barely heard it, and what I did hear did not make sense. A round of applause was followed by no one stepping forward to collect their award. No, never, this is not true. This does not happen to me. Well believe it or not, it had, and it had happened right there, right now. Cautiously, I apologised to fellow attendees as I tried to shuffle forward through the packed room, twisting sideways to reach the middle of the gallery.

The Mayor again stated what this painting meant to the jury and why it had been selected for what I then realised was the Lannion Award. He stated that he hoped that they had picked the right painting. Cheekily, I could not help saying to him "You did," much to the laughter of the guests.

An exhilarating moment indeed. I felt humbled. The guidance given by Paul Wakefield at the beginning of the week and the subsequent accolade bestowed on me made me think. I had jumped at the opportunity for that meeting, just as I had once more pushed the negativity in me to one side, entered this competition and been part of the subsequent awards event.

Sometimes, fortune does favour the brave.

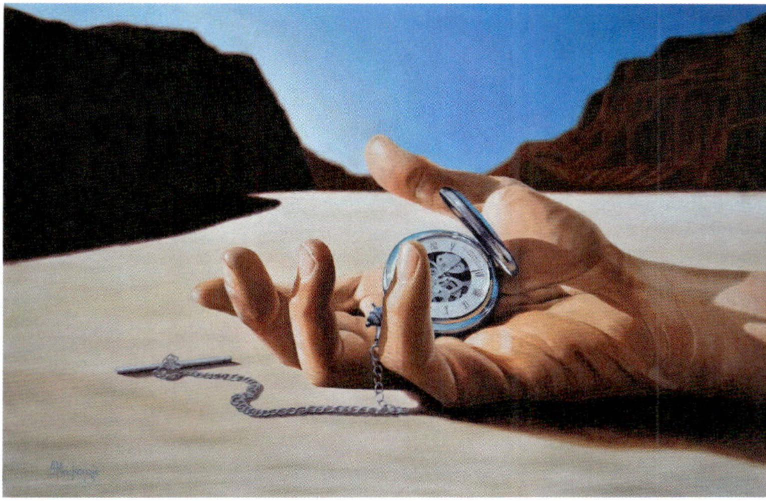

Once Upon a Time in the West II 76 x 51cm
by Ian Mackenzie

28

"When you bring me out, can you introduce me as Joker?"

Every time I pick up a paint brush or I have an idea in my head for a new piece of artwork, I have a desire to make this the very best piece to date. Whether this is an animal, much loved and lost, or an image that will tell a story, the subject is irrelevant. This next artwork will be the best I can achieve.

I am unsure sometimes where ideas come from. However, once an image has appeared, it can lead to all sorts of interesting and thought-provoking concepts. Some of these are pretty simple and straight forward, and some are intricate and hold detailed and deep-seated meanings.

With my recent artwork, I have been interested in where the idea has come from. I have asked myself, what does this potential artwork mean to me and how will others interpret it?

As previously mentioned, on occasions, I will speak to people, usually friends who are a little quirky and also openminded in their thoughts and approach to life. I will entice their feelings and ideas on a subject that usually enrich my latest project. I will expand the idea and add more to it and see what develops. I will dig deep into my experiences and ask myself why am I going to paint this and where has this idea come from?

This process can soon lead to so many more possibilities to consider. At times, I need to reign in the ideas and focus on one single image that I want from it. With the other options, I add them to my ideas notebook for future artwork and try to focus on the piece in hand before expanding them further. This can be quite difficult, as sometimes my mind is off running with all sorts of images and ideas. However, I am very fortunate to be creative in this way and thankful that I can transfer this to different activities and help others with their creativeness.

In the case of the Joker, I am not sure how or where the idea came from initially. As I questioned myself, all sorts of ideas started to evolve. Each one had its own story that came from experiences I had lived through years before. The different combinations of characters were fascinating.

It became an intriguing process to ask myself how on earth I was coming up with ideas that could potentially be so controversial, I could not possibly paint them. The characters were so strong and in their individual way, they related back to me and my life.

In thinking back, it was one sunny morning when I was just leaving a close friend's house, when I had the flash of inspiration. We had been spending time talking of the skulduggery and activity around our old job, now that we had both retired. Stephen Rhys Williams, known to us by the nickname of Twm, had worked with me within the Police Unit at the

National Assembly for Wales for years. He had helped me to create the links with the Welsh Government and respective Ministers. He was worth his weight in gold and being six foot four inches tall and the son of a British Lions rugby legend, that was a lot of gold.

Again, we had been laughing at the situations we used to find ourselves in with politicians. Some were of our own doing and some were totally random acts of bizarreness that you could not make up yourself. Being close to the Ministers and their staff revealed another world that a lot do not see and most care very little about. But that is the beauty of the political world. It is never short of characters, opinions, political disasters and victories, and of course the occasional scandal. It is a huge back catalogue of information and intrigue to one day turn into thought provoking art, perhaps.

As I left my friend's home, I mentioned that I had this idea to combine two characters and paint a portrait of them coming together in one face. I mentioned who they would be as I left, and started thinking why I was creating this image, and what was making me think of it. He laughed as I revealed who they were, and we started to comment on all sorts of connotations.

The fantastic film 'The Joker' starring Joaquin Phoenix, had me hooked from the very first trailer I saw. This was different, unlike all the other superhero films of the last decade. This was a very dark character who had been played by many actors in recent times, but none like this. I saw the film and I was absolutely blown away. This was not the high glossy imagery of the modern take on hero versus villain, with so much fast-moving CGI, you never know where to look and end up missing half of the scenes.

This was the story of the demise of a person through bullying, misfortune and through his mental health. As far as I was concerned, this was the real story. The affects on a lowly placed individual in society, never able to really grasp the concept of the world around him, and not given the chance to do so either, created a character that only had one way in life, one direction, one path. And that was downhill.

At the same time as this film hit our screens, we had another character in our midst. A person filling the media every day. No matter where we went, he was there on our screens, in our newspapers, instructing us and being constantly quoted no matter where we were. Boris Johnson was going places, and there was no stopping him. He had been prevented in the past, but now his vision was clear, his direction uninterrupted, and he was going to be our next Prime Minister. His path was on the way up.

So, two characters, one fictitious and one real, albeit some may argue this point, but both having an impact on us in different ways. The rise of a future leader not without his own personal issues and battles, smashing his way through the Brexit deadlock like a true Stan Lee character, to finally hold the highest political post in the land. And of course, the everyday man fighting off his downward spiralling mental health, depicted in the finest cinematic film seen that year.

Somewhere in the middle, they needed to meet. The compromise between the rise and fall, the rich and poor, supreme power and nothing. Somehow, the two must come together and blend into one face, one body, one being. And there was no better way to do this than through the art of oil paint on canvas.

The result of this creation caused emotions on both sides of the political spectrum. I experienced praise and adulation at such a creative piece of artwork. I also witnessed arguments on social media when I posted the work, and I received suggestive comments that I needed to create paintings of politicians from the other side, with similar ridicule to match.

I knew then that my art had done something more than just fill a gap on the wall or brighten up a dull room in a house. It had triggered exactly what I wanted it to. It was starting to evoke, challenge and inspire.

Other combinations had come to mind once I had the basis of this piece. In fact, a few ideas I had would not only evoke, challenge and inspire others, they would really question my character in turning them into pieces of artwork themselves. Could I push this subject right to the brink, I had to ask myself?

Two pieces in particular came to mind and reflected the current media hype within society. The first concerned the Labour Party and their previous leader Jeremy Corbyn, embroiled in his controversial dealings with the Jewish community. Take a picture of him and one of the dress code of an orthodox Jewish male, combine them and you will have the image I was thinking of.

The second centred on a member of the Royal Family and his alleged activity with the young guests of a financier and convicted sex offender. I will leave you guess how this one could look.

Both portraits will one day be painted, they have to be. But right now, I had a further idea based on the particular character I had created.

"When you bring me out, can you introduce me as Joker?" was born.

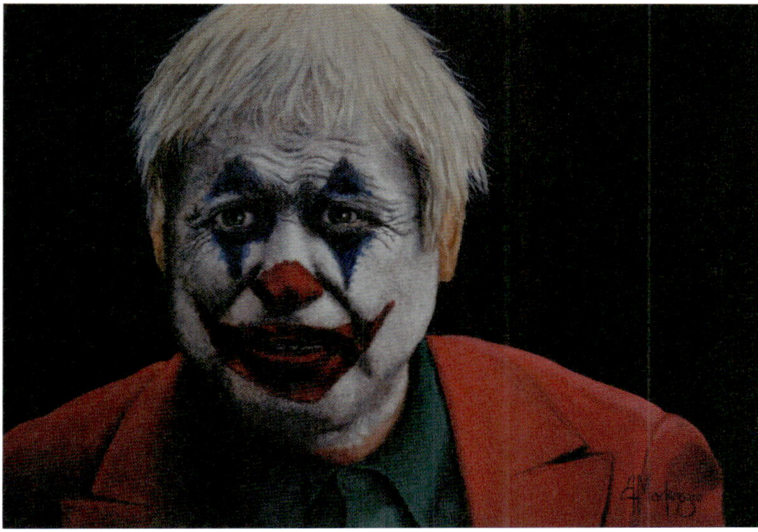

"When you bring me out, can you introduce me as Joker?"
33 x 25cm by Ian Mackenzie

29

"Is it just me, or is it getting crazier out there?"

Well I could not stop there. I was on a roll. There was something in this I thought. As I talked to people about this idea, they were intrigued.

The new Prime Minister Boris Johnson had just given his inaugural speech on the steps of Number 10 Downing Street. My mind raced. He concluded, waved, and turned towards the front door, entering as the leader and the future of our country.

As the months rolled on, the world went mad. Floods swept across the nation wrecking homes, villages and businesses that could not defend themselves. Brexit continued to divide families, friends and communities, as other countries distanced themselves from us. Covid-19 took hold in a horrendously devastating manner and ripped into the lives of everyone, infecting and killing randomly as it spread. And the Black Lives Matter movement came to the forefront identifying grassroot issues, as protests turned violent.

My mind went back to the image of Boris turning one last time before entering his new home. Wasn't there a quote from the film 'The Joker' that summed up this eclectic picture of hysteria, worry and uncertainty?

I had posted the last painting of Boris as the Joker on social media, and it had received some excellent comments and attracted a lot of attention. I knew it was current and this theme was one which could be expanded. I could either go with the ideas of creating another character based on two prominent figures or paint another Joker. In looking back over the clips from the film, it was obvious. The world was crazy on the outside, one man had the future of the country to manage, rivers to dam, Brexit to clear up, new alliances to form, Covid-19 to eradicate, a massive debt like never before, and a worrying surge of discourse ripping through the ideology that once made this country powerful.

Yes, the Prime Minister turning and entering Number 10 was the one. Shut the door and all those problems are no more than a distant image on the TV that can be switched off and forgotten about.

I would not wish it on anyone. It was enough to push even the strongest over the edge.

The title "Is it just me, or is it getting crazier out there?" fitted the image so well.

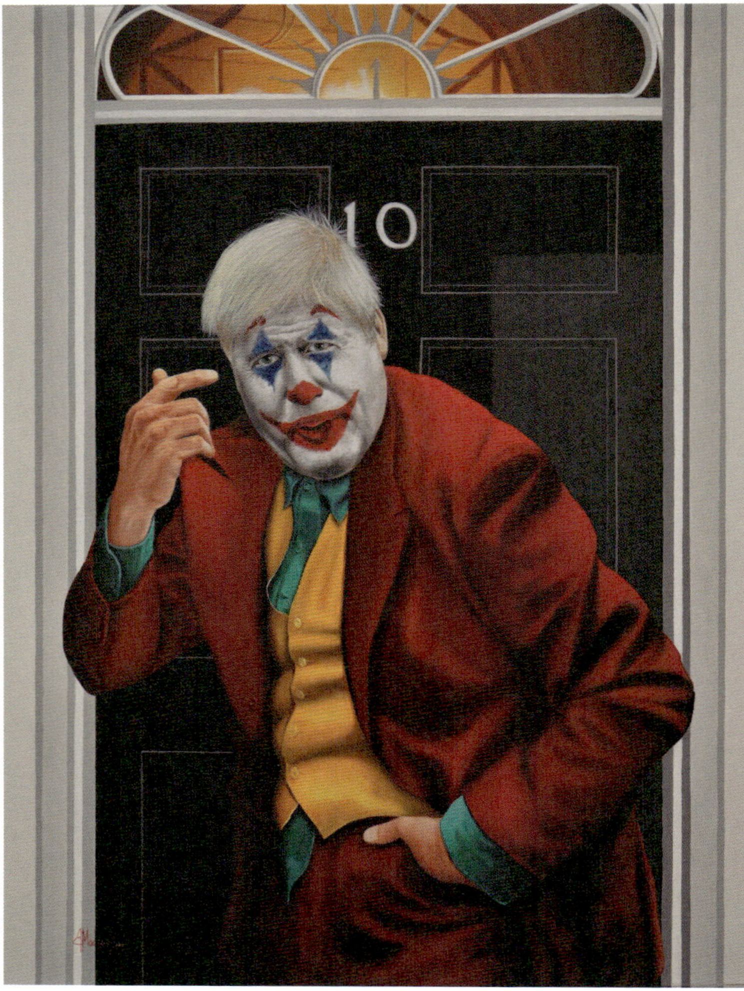

“Is it just me, or is it getting crazier out there?” 76 x 102cm
by Ian Mackenzie

30

"What Have We Done?"

There are two ways to look at a piece of artwork. One is to be told the story behind why it was created and let that interpretation inform you about what you are looking at. The other is to stand in front of the piece and see what you want to see from the image facing you. This is the beauty of art, as both have their place, and both can be enlightening.

I hope that in this book I can convey to you, the reader, why I have painted certain people and paintings, and what I was thinking at the time of creating the work. It is my passion and desire to grab those images that flash before me and try with the best will in the world to get them down on canvas, to tell a story that has meaning and purpose.

If you are looking at a painting and trying to understand it, go for it, as there is nothing stopping you. It may be the colours that have drawn you to it, or the subject itself that has appealed to you. You may not come to the same conclusion as the artist had when they started painting it, but what you want to see could be much more important for you than the artist's original intention.

Each of us has walked a different path and experienced a unique journey. It is that collection of knowledge that influences how we see others, and possibly informs us when we look at art.

As far as I am aware, I was the only teenage Rod Stewart fan in punk clothing, queuing outside Buffalo Records on the Hayes in Cardiff, on the day of the release of his new album, who in time got beaten up, became a highly graded karate practitioner, faced dangerous and life threatening situations weekly, carried a gun in the police, and subsequently kept politicians out of trouble. I am still nervous and lack confidence. Therefore, in considering this, I do have a different view to others about people and the world of art.

My place is not to find fault with what others see in paintings and what enjoyment they take from it, regardless of my own interpretation of what they are looking at and my own personal likes and dislikes. In fact, it is the opposite and in particular with reference to my own art I am intrigued with how people interpret it and what they say. I must admit that I have been known to steal a description or two from people commenting on my work, as they are far more sophisticated accounts than I could ever come up with.

It does not matter if you do not understand what the artist is trying to portray in their artwork. What matters is that you enjoy what you are looking at, or at least you experience it and take what is necessary from it for yourself.

There is no better example of this than my painting called "What Have We Done?". Viewers experiences and what they have been exposed to in life show in their different interpretations of what this painting stands for.

I showed this artwork to a few separate people recently. When they realized that the model was wrapped in a black and white Union Jack flag, they came to a conclusion that was different to their first interpretation. They all said that this painting, with the flag itself being black, represented the change in the country and was a reference to the Black Lives Matter movement. Their interpretation was very current.

A strong message indeed and if this is the message taken from this by another, then so be it. Mine is not to argue against this, just as a song and its lyrics will mean something to one person and mean something totally different to someone else.

However, this painting is actually about Brexit, and the demise of the Union Jack. The once great flag in its colour and glory stood high and proud, probably the most famous flag in the world, representing the vastness of the British Empire stretching from Hong Kong to Canada. Over time, countries have wriggled from the grasp of the nation and its dominance and have broken free from its historical hold. In turn, the four nations within our isles too have struggled with the urge of independence.

Of course, the UKs' fight to be released from the shackles of Europe have very much dominated recent times. Most disturbingly, this move has divided the nation right down the middle and driven hard into the fabric of our country, both sides of the political sphere and our economic future. There has been so much turmoil within the country, that we do not know which way to look. We have turned in on ourselves with a sense of impending doom. What have we done to ourselves as a nation to allow this to happen? There lies the title of this painting.

The flag losing its colour and vitality, turning dark and sinister, representing a menacing evil that has infested our very existence running through our veins, through the streets and into every brick and structure of the foundation of our homeland. Brexit, for good or for evil, has brought out the worst in us, with protests on both sides of the argument, political spin, extortionate costs, immigration, borders, NHS funding and dissent at the highest level, to name a few, tearing us apart as a nation.

"What Have We Done?" depicts this struggle. But in terms of the beauty of art being seen by others with their own interpretation, it can very well be a reference to Black Lives Matter.

If someday, someone delves deeper into this painting's construction, they will no doubt find a further twist to its story.

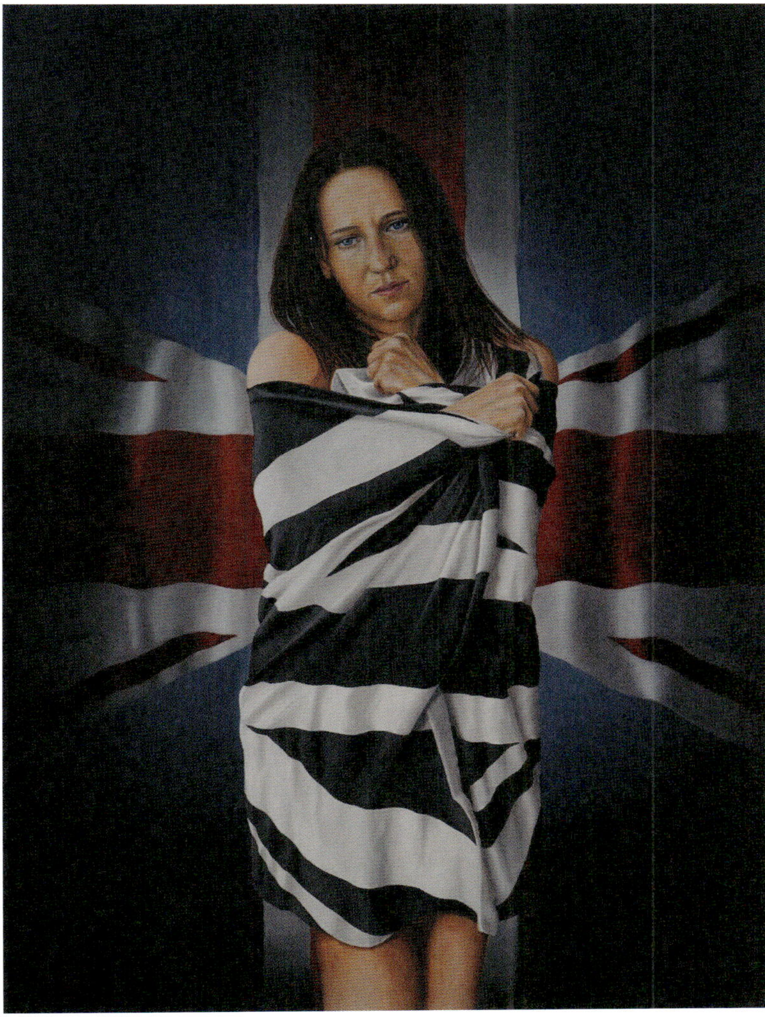

"What Have We Done?" 76 x 101cm by Ian Mackenzie

31

The Profit

Finally, I leave you with one of my paintings that has caused a considerable stir on social media. Maybe not as much controversy as the actual subject has caused in his time in office, but this subject has proved a revelation. Politics is a hot bed of debate and discourse, and currently there is absolutely no let-up whatsoever. Every person has an opinion, the media publicise the extremes, and the political world stretches its boundaries each waking day.

There is not a script writer who could come up with a more intricate plot or shocking headline. It is a haven for those artistic individuals who only need to combine a couple of ideas or take a notion that one step further, or even just replicate what they actually see in front of them, and they have enough material to create an entertaining subject for the world to view. That subject becomes the artwork which in turn tells a story, and as I have alluded to in previous chapters, there are currently a lot of stories to tell.

As you look at this image in particular, I have a story of why and how I created this painting in oils on canvas. Mine is one story. Without me telling you it, you will have your own story of this painting of what it means to you, which will be of equal value to my story. Maybe in coming together, we will have the same story.

Maybe in reading my book, you too will have had similar experiences as I have had in life and will want to share those with others in a form that you are comfortable with.

And maybe, just maybe, this painting tells the story itself and needs no explanation. If so, my job as the Storytelling Artist is complete.

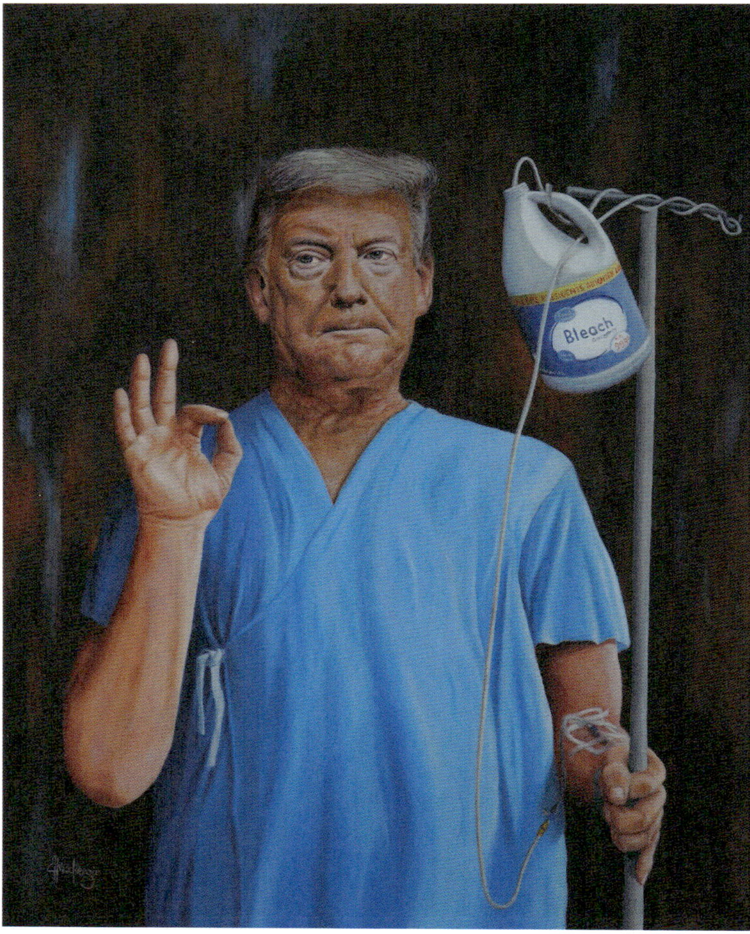

The Profit 61 x 76cm by Ian Mackenzie

Part Six

And Finally

32

Never Give Up On A Dream

A friend came to see my art recently. When I revealed my latest project, he was as excited as I was when I started creating it. He said, "If you had been given better advice in school, and had taken art further, think where you would be now in the art world."

It certainly made me pause for thought and reflect on what might have been and where I might have ended up. However, it made me realize more than ever, I would not have wanted to change anything in the journey that I had experienced. It had culminated at this point today, with a talent that I am grateful for, and artwork that has brought happiness to many people.

His statement made me think back of all the experiences that I have related in this book. One in particular came to mind and I questioned myself about it. Would I have wanted to avoid that callous attack in that night club when I was sixteen years old? It would have certainly saved me a lot of mental anguish and stress in the following years, no doubt.

Perhaps I would not have lost as much confidence as I did, had I not been attacked. However, I was never the most confident or outgoing person to start with. Mind you, it would have certainly saved my brand new frilly red shift from being ripped; I know that for sure.

Nevertheless, had I not experienced the physical pain and subsequent mental anguish of that attack, I would have not sought solace in learning karate. Thirty-eight years of training and counting would be totally different. I would probably have not felt the urge and desire to join the police, and of course I would not have had any of the experiences of society, the drama, the anguish and excitement to tell in stories, let alone impart them on to canvas in the form of controversial and luxury art.

I would not be where I am now and would not have found the fantastic friends and met the influential people who have come to shape my world, my journey, and my art.

For those reasons, I would not want to change what happened to me one bit. Whether it was the lack of support for a career in art and the misguided direction, or the attack by heartless older males, picking on someone who looked different, both situations have played an incredible part in making me who I am today.

I now have a solid structure of concepts and situations to form a basis for potential artwork that excites me beyond all imagination. I have an awareness of people's behaviour and the cruelness they can sink to. I have skills and strategies to help, in some way at least, to overcome my lack of confidence, which still haunts me today, and I have the desire to succeed in helping others with similar problems. Furthermore, my wish to achieve success in the world of art is greater now than at any other time before.

So, with this in mind, if in reading my story you have identified with certain parts of this book, and it has struck a chord with your own difficulties and the uncertainties you have faced in life, or you want to succeed in your choice of lifestyle and change what you have right now, I have a challenge for you.

Whatever the circumstances that have led to this moment, they have occurred. They are definitely in the past. You cannot change them. They may be deeply entrenched in negativity and bad feelings, but they are part of you and will inform your decision-making process until you die. So, you might as well use them to your own benefit.

Think about what you are now going to do about the rest of your life or what you want to change to make a difference for you: no one else, you. And start preparing for change by grabbing your dream idea with both hands. The negativity may have driven you down or the lack of an opportunity may have binned your dream, but that gut feeling you had when it happened and may still have, will now form your sole focus for success.

Write your dream down in a simple sentence. Identify a couple of people who are positive or quirky in their outlook and tell them what your dream is. The first step of success has now been achieved. Make a small list of how you are going to get to your dream, and cross off your first task of telling someone. Believe it or not, the actual crossing off the first task is in itself very satisfying.

Do not sit in a chair or lie in bed and wait for the motivation to come to you to take you towards your dream. It will not. You have to physically get up and walk towards your next task. So, tell yourself to get up, and actually get up. One step at a time, tick off each stage from your list, and your motivation will come. Your desire to achieve your goal or dream will take over and motivation will be second nature.

Tell someone of the anguish you have felt, the problems you have faced and subsequently of your plight and your dream. Ask them to look out for you on your journey and join in with support and positive advice. If they are true to you, they will. If they are not, put them to one side, as there are plenty of positive people who will take their place and support you. They are out there waiting for you to tell them your plan for your dream.

Keep reminding yourself that people who achieve the greatest are not the most talented in their field. They are the ones with the motivation and the desire. Those that wait and pontificate in order to gain perfection will still be sat waiting when you run past them full pelt towards your dream, leaving them in the distance behind, laughing at the perpetual motion and the snowball effect of your motivation and desire that you and you alone have created.

Embrace your difference from the mainstream and place it alongside your willingness to commit to your journey. You look or act differently because you think differently. Exploit it for your creativity. It is your greatest strength. Look for friends who are also different, as well as those who are inconspicuous. They hold fantastic ideas that will set your imagination on fire.

And of course, document your journey. You never know when that itself will come in use, when someone else will want to know about how you did it, or when you will want to help others in their struggle and their dream.

So, what are you waiting for?

For me, my journey is far from over. I now have one or two more things to cross off my list and I will admit to doing so with a little inner satisfaction. I am flawed and I still lack confidence. However, I do believe that my motivation and desire mask this inability and helps me run as fast as I possibly can towards what I am trying to achieve. I hope that it will see me through as it has to date, and I thoroughly recommend it without hesitation.

On reflection, I now see that it was my hunger for revenge I referred to in a previous chapter that became my desire to succeed. It developed into an all-consuming need to survive physically and mentally. It gave me my strength to endure all types of degrading behaviour and turn a lot of experiences to my advantage.

I am grateful for everything that has happened to me, from my upbringing and my family, to my career and all the friends I have made, and the chances to experience life from many different perspectives.

I hope that along this journey I am taking I can inspire someone and maybe guide them, as I was guided by kind and thoughtful people and I continue to be guided by them and others to this day.

In terms of my art, in a selfish way, I must admit that I would like to enjoy some recognition for my artwork whilst I am alive, rather than immense fame when I am dead!

My dream is to exhibit artwork at the Halcyon Gallery in London alongside work by Mitch Griffiths, who is to me the most influential contemporary artist I have experienced. From the moment I saw his exhibition 'The Promised Land' in 2010, I knew without a doubt my ambition. I had no idea of the route it would take, but from that date on my desire and motivation were set.

With that in mind, it is my wish and my aim to create iconic pieces of art that represent our lives, our society, and our world. I do not want to hold back or be held back by anyone or anything. I want to show people from all walks of life that art can represent them, and it can capture their troubles and their ambition. It can tell their story like no other way.

I want to be able to place these pieces of artwork in the best galleries that there are, so the rich, the famous and influential see my stories on canvas of the plight of the downtrodden, the abused and forgotten.

So, there you have it. My story, my aim, and my intention of never giving up on a dream. It has been one hell of an adventure so far and it feels like I haven't even started. There are many mountains to climb and more downhill slopes to ride.

Come with me, and be part of my no holds barred, no Plan B, and never giving up journey through my art. What have you got to lose?

Ian Mackenzie

www.ianmackenzieart.co.uk

ian@ianmackenzieart.co.uk

https://www.facebook.com/ianmackenzieart

https://www.instagram.com/ianmackenzieart

About the Author

Ian Mackenzie started creating artwork at an early age, demonstrating his skill of perspective, colour and shape. Coming from a terraced street in a coastal town in Wales, UK, he enjoyed the freedoms of young life.

However, circumstances took him from his talent, his journey created for him by others. Nevertheless, he commenced a successful and rewarding thirty-year career as a Police Officer involved with crime, public order, terrorism and the world of politicians.

For his last ten years of service, he was the Officer in Charge of the National Assembly for Wales Police Unit and has safeguarded politicians, Prime Ministers, and members of both foreign and UK Royal Families, including the Queen.

He has recently come full circle back to his talent and now brings a complete life of experiences and stories to create luxury art that evokes, challenges and inspires people's emotions.

He has exhibited at numerous galleries in Wales and surrounding area and is constantly sought after for luxury commissioned artwork. His creativity has been recognized several times and he recently won Y Galeri Caerphilly Open Art 2020 Lannion Award.

His life has taken him from victim to 5th Dan Black Belt, the highest grade awarded in his karate organization, and now beyond, with his creativity and his stories being told through his luxury art.

He lives in South Wales, UK and you can visit him online at

www.ianmackenzieart.co.uk

Printed in Poland
by Amazon Fulfillment
Poland Sp. z o.o., Wrocław

66380605R00114